The

Beauty

of

a

God Box

A Little Book and a Little Box—That Will Do Big Things

by

Mark Joseph Martinez

For permission requests, email the publisher, addressed "Attention: Copyright Coordinator," at manifestwithgodnow@gmail.com
Little Books Publishing Company

This book is a work of non-fiction. Any opinions, findings, conclusions, or recommendations expressed in this work are those of the author and do not necessarily reflect the views of the publisher.

Library of Congress Cataloging-in-Publication Data
Registration Number TXu 2-361-765
Effective date of Registration February 23, 2023
Registration Decision Date: March 28, 2023

Acknowledgments

I write these words with deep gratitude and an overwhelming sense of indebtedness. However, no words, gestures, or deeds could ever fully convey the depth of my thanks for what the following people have contributed to my life.

First, my never-ending gratitude must be extended to the three most important women in my life: my mom, Bea Ann Garcia, who now rests with God; my wife, Christie, whose inspiration has enriched my life; my daughter, Monique, whose radiant spirit continues to illuminate my path.

This is for Mickey. Just as you taught Christie. *The Beauty of a God Box*

To Aunt Belinda, Uncle Eddie, and Uncle Rick, I extend my heartfelt thanks and a love that knows no bounds. Your care for my mother during times when I could not be there has left an indelible mark on my heart, and for that, I will forever be in your debt.

I also want to express special gratitude to two remarkable women who played pivotal roles in bringing this book to life beyond my wildest imagination. To my dear friend Chris, who tirelessly worked on the first draft, enabling the world to hear this story. And to Jessica Marshall, who skillfully transformed the words of a son, father, and husband into a thoughtfully organized, beautiful piece of literature. Your contributions have made an immeasurable impact on this work.

To all of you who have impacted my life, thank you.

Mark Joseph Martinez

From the Beginning
to the end,
all the Glory Goes to
God

A Note to My Readers

Now that I use a God Box, I no longer look at what the world needs to change to make me happy. I look at what needs to be changed within me to make the world a better place.

I authored this book to bring hope to others who need God to do the impossible. You see, not so long ago, I was probably a lot like you, or maybe the person you're most worried for in your life right now—I was alone and scared. I fought addictions to drugs and alcohol. My daughter disowned me. I had no place to live. At rock bottom, I gave up on God.

But I had something going in my life, whether or not I knew it at the time: God never gave up on me. Once I used a God Box, my life changed beyond finances, housing, and relationships. It gave me peace of mind I never knew attainable. I am called to share this with all of you believing that no matter what your struggle is, your God and a God Box will change your life.

God bless you on this journey.

Mark Joseph Martinez

*Time to get Started
Let God be Your Guide*

Contents

Introduction

I will never forget the day my mom killed my father with love. That man dropped dead from a simple gesture of her kindness, a single act that came from her heart. Long before that, in the middle of their terrible divorce, he beat her so severely that he put her into a coma. He terrorized her for at least ten years after the divorce was finalized She killed my father, and her abuser, years later with a kiss.

But this book is not about my life. It isn't about my parents' lives either. Though I promise, if you stick through to the end of this book, I'll tell you the whole story of my father's death. For now, let's get down to business.

A God Box works for those who need help, be it for themselves or others, fulfilling needs physically, emotionally, mentally, and spiritually. This book can help you get more money, a bigger house, a new car, or a newfound love with another or of yourself. No matter what drew you to this book, a God Box will change your life. How do I know? It has and continues to work for me and many others. I'm confident it will work for you.

Putting your hopes and dreams into a God Box might sound scary, or maybe even silly. Perhaps you're already thinking that nothing will work for you and your unique situation. Let me assure you, thousands of others have trusted this method, and their results were meaningful changes, unexpected opportunities, and lasting serenity. God has blessed me and others repeatedly, and now it's your turn.

Before I ever heard about a God Box, all I knew of were wish or manifestation boxes. The way I understood them to work was this: You put a picture of a Tesla Model X Plaid in the wish box and one magically appears. No work to do, no God to trust in—just voila! A dream come true! I didn't quite comprehend how the wish box got you that car. Does a genie come out of the box and grant you three wishes? A magic blue fairy? Maybe a leprechaun?

With a God Box, I know who is in charge: God.

I learned how to use a God Box from my wife, Christie. She learned it from her dear friend, Mickey. Mickey learned it in a twelve-step program from a woman who taught it to her. This is generally how the tradition of a God Box has been passed throughout the years, from one person's lips to another's heart. Mickey taught Christie when she struggled with situations out of her control. Christie wrote down on paper the person, place, or principle interfering with her serenity. She dropped that slip of paper into a cardboard box originally containing a pair of shoes that she'd labeled "God Box," then forgot about it. As Mickey instructed, Christie left it to God to handle, righten, or fix. And she still does. Whatever is too difficult to handle or is out of Christie's control gets scrawled onto a page and dropped in her God Box. For her, a God Box is a direct phone line to God.

The God Box worked wonders for my wife. She doesn't worry about money, people, or situations. With a little nudge from God (yes, God!), I decided to try it.

At that time, I was worried about my brother, Paul. He lived in a group home that assisted people with mental and physical issues. He wasn't happy there. Paul's situation was out of my control; the doctor told me he was self-sufficient and could handle his own affairs. I felt differently since my phone was ringing with calls informing me Paul wasn't going to his medical appointments. He depended on me for his clothes, cigarettes, and companionship. Why couldn't I make decisions for him? Yes, he was a grown man, but he still had emotional and mental needs. In particular, Paul had trouble with decision making when left to his own devices.

Doctors and therapists could not discuss his condition with me without his consent. I wasn't allowed to make them move him somewhere else. I didn't have the money for Paul to have his own private residence. I just kept thinking, *If I were in control, Paul's life would be better*.

Many sleepless nights, I pictured my brother mistreated and neglected. My mind conjured various worse-case scenarios. I overcompensated for the times I wasn't there for him. The worry took its toll on me. Incessant anxiety and frustration impacted my health. I needed to open myself up to new ideas in order to stop the fear. I love my brother and wanted what was best for him. I asked my wife, Christie, for help. She told me to try a God Box and explained how to make one. She instructed me to write my brother's name on a slip of paper and put it in the God Box. I did as I was told with no expectations or hope of real results. How could I believe anything would change? All I did was add a piece of paper with my brother Paul's name into this so-called God Box. Not a genie nor fairy nor leprechaun popped out, and for sure, no Teslas appeared in the driveway.

I love to run the show. I want to play the hero. I want to play God. I know better than others who—without question—are more qualified than me. I subconsciously or consciously think, *Don't they know who I am?* If I'm not in control of a situation, nobody should be, especially God. But there I was using what I thought was a cute idea because I was suffering from something I had no control over.

God showed me it was more than a cute idea. It worked. Days later, my brother's problem resolved itself without my help. Paul found a place to live that he liked and frankly, he was happy as hell. I better say happy as heck. I am sure my spiritual advisor Dustin would advise me to watch the language. Who knew a little piece of paper in a box could change my brother's world along with my own? The obsession and worry over Paul's welfare ended with no effort needed from me. The situation managed to fix itself. Somehow, I let it go and gave it to God, unbeknownst to myself.

It felt and seemed like magic. At the time, I couldn't tell you why it worked. It did, and that's all I needed to know. It worked so well that I decided to try it with car issues, money problems, and family discord. Of course, Christie suggested I put my mental and emotional issues in a God Box months before, but I resisted—until I was at my wit's end with Paul's troubles and I finally gave in. I could have saved myself from so much needless worry if I had only listened to my dear wife sooner. I could have used that energy I wasted on useful things. God's favor and gifts could have come quicker. But thankfully I had the good sense to listen eventually, and I got to work.

I compiled my necessities and desires:

- My daughter, Monique (she was not speaking with me, and I knew it was my fault)

- Worry over money

- Names of people who annoyed the heck out of me

- My mental and emotional needs

- Food

- Warrants out for my arrest (misdemeanor warrants; three in total)

- Write a book

- Help staying clean and sober

- God, I need your help to be a better person

- A car, savings, and lots of friends would be cool

I wrote all these issues (and more) that I needed help with on paper, hoping God could manage them better than I had. My wants and needs, my goals and aspirations, material goodies I wanted—grab a pen or pencil and put them on paper. Names of people I thought wronged me—on a piece of paper. Fears and struggles, dreams and whims, big problems and minor irritations—all in graphite and ink in a rectangular cube with the words "God Box" on it, and the rest as they say, is history.

My life transformed in ways I never could have believed or imagined. Issues resolved themselves. Gifts came from God. God showed me favor and love. Then came the bonus. I was blessed with material objects; I did not deserve these things but received them from God. I no longer worried over things that used to hold me hostage. I no longer suffered from depression and mental illness. I had no reason to worry about my next meal. God did for me what no person had ever been able to do including me: He took control over my unmanageable life.

God and the God Box helped me gain money, property, and well-being. It helped me become a man of integrity and love. I now experience financial and emotional stability in ways I never thought possible. You want specifics? Sure you do. I don't blame you, and I hate to disappoint (I want to be the hero, remember?).

A few years ago, Christie and I were living together here in Albuquerque, unmarried at the time, with no vehicle. She bummed rides, walked, or took the bus to work. I hopped downtown on the bus to attend my mental, physical, and emotional rehabilitation appointments at Health Care for the Homeless.

Christie and I needed a car. We didn't have money to put down on one and our credit scores were nonexistent at best. A car was out of the question. An acquaintance, let's call him Tom, that my wife and I interacted with occasionally, went out on his own and found a car he thought we might like. Tom showed the car to us, and he bought the vehicle and let us make payments we could afford to him. He charged no interest, and there were no strings attached.

Talk about stunned. I'm still pinching myself to see if it was real (ow! —but yeah, it's still parked in the driveway). Karma tells me I do not deserve good people in my life. My past deeds should have me doomed to endless pain and misery. No way do I deserve forgiveness, support, help, or gifts from God. Good deeds don't happen to someone like me. God and my God Box did not see it that way. I don't know whether God spoke directly to Tom or gave him an intuitive spiritual thought. All I know is that my wife and I no longer need to walk or bum rides or take buses as a direct result of letting go and giving it to God and a box.

All these miracles and blessings I and countless others experience are a result of a God Box. I will show you how God and His Box restored my sanity. I was delusional and suffered from severe depression. God, good people, and my God Box changed that.

It would be selfish to keep to myself what was freely given to me. God wants me to share this simple act, so God can help you discern, understand, and focus on what you need or want. God wants everyone—including you—to have love, peace, and compassion.

No matter how big your dream, no matter how small the request, whatever situation you are in today, it can change for the better. No crazy procedures are needed. There are no magical words or rituals. Simply write down what you need God to intercede with on your behalf, and place it in your God Box. Watch how your life changes.

No matter what God you follow, this book will help you. No need to pray over the God Box. You certainly can if it brings you comfort and joy, but it's not required. It doesn't matter what religious doctrine you follow or what name you call your Higher Power. Whatever you choose to call God—the Spirit of the Universe, Creator, Allah, Jehovah, Jesus, She, Gaia, Shanti, or so many more—most of us acknowledge there is a Great Power at work in our universe in some fashion. I happen to call this Power, "God." In this book, I use the gender-neutral form of the pronoun "He" or "Him" to refer to the God of my understanding. Feel free to mentally replace your Power's name or pronouns how you see fit.

This book can work for you no matter where you are in your walk with God. It will help you form a more meaningful connection with your God. You will get closer to God and your dreams in ways you never thought possible. God will be in control of your life. The box is a symbol of God. God will manifest and set in motion what needs to happen to let His gifts arrive. Peace and serenity will become second nature.

Whether a true believer or a weekend warrior for God, whether you pray on your knees every night, only in foxholes, or have never whispered a word you'd consider in that vein, it does not matter. God can and will do for you the impossible.

A God Box does not require you to stop practicing what your God asks of you. Continue to honor or obey the God of your understanding. Kneel, bow, stand, shout, dance, sing, and do what God moves you to do with your faith or spirituality. I love to pray and go to church. I also love to see people worship in their own ways. In this book, we will not talk about prayer or religious practices. You request what you want and need. Then God provides you with the gift—the only requirement is faith.

One favor I ask—and I know what you're thinking—*Here comes the sales pitch.* No, that isn't what this is. I only ask this: Once you experience the abundance God has for you, please share this book and how God blesses you with others. A simple act of kindness, a smile, an expression of the hope and joy you feel within will do just fine! Let others know what God and the God Box have done for you. Help others live in a world full of love and tolerance. Spread the wealth of love and compassion. Share what you learn in this book. God's light shines brighter on those who get excited and share what God has freely given them.

Information you need to know and remember:

- My mom killed her ex-husband, my dad, with love. We will learn more about that later.

- I was the guy you saw digging out of trashcans before I found God and a God Box.

- Now I'm a guy who helps other drug addicts and drunks find a better way to live.

- A God Box will change your life in ways you never imagined.

- I, like you, want to be in control of everyone, everything, and all situations.

- With a God Box, you can let go of those things out of your control.

- You can use a God Box for peace, love, and serenity. My wife uses hers for good mental health.

- I use my God Box to get material possessions like cars, a house, and cash. Why wouldn't I?

- When you reap the benefits, give back to others. A God Box gives more when you give back.

Those are the broad strokes, folks. As you read, you'll learn more about me and people I've known, the hard times I went through and the miracles I witnessed. But before we dive in, I think there's a story you need to hear.

You see, I wasn't always the man I am today. I didn't feel too kindly towards God, but this story proves he always had my best interest in mind. I want you to know He was looking out for me nonetheless, just like he's looking out for you, no matter how you feel about Him.

It was early in my sobriety, three weeks tops. The pandemic was in full swing, and people showed their true colors. Who fights over toilet paper? We do. Although clean and sober, I suffered from delusions and depression to the point of suicidal ideation. A constant thought— that I was not worthy of living because of my past actions—raced like a hamster on a wheel, and that hamster was working overtime. I met with a group of drunks every day who were all staying sober, but I was hanging on only by the tips of my fingers.

A disco ball hung from the ceiling in the room we met in and there was a piano in one corner. A podium stood tall at the front of the room for folks to speak. The dual-handle coffee pots perpetually brewed an alcoholic's finest ambrosia, Folgers Classic Roast. The smokey, almost-burnt, flowery aroma still overwhelms me whenever I walk into that room where my friends and I still meet.

That room with the disco ball and the scent of Folgers Classic is where I met David and Anna, a free-spirited couple who drove down from San Francisco on a whim to Albuquerque. David quickly became one of my closest friends. He told me how he and Anna attended art therapy at Albuquerque Health Care for the Homeless (AHCH). I was not technically homeless, and I mean no disrespect to my brothers and sisters out on the street, but I looked and smelled like I had no home to shower in. I had trouble holding my bowels and regularly peed in my pants from alcohol and drug withdrawals. In short, I was a stinky mess.

David told me he and Anna went twice a week for three hours to art therapy, and nobody but them attended due to COVID-19. He said I should take a ride with them to AHCH and check it out. David explained I could get therapy there as well as attend the art therapy class. I was down to try just about anything. My mental illness had taken its toll on me. I was ready to snap at society or myself. I couldn't take another day of living like I was.

I couldn't focus and didn't know what to do with my emotions now I no longer had alcohol or drugs to turn to. I would have physically hurt someone or myself if I didn't get help soon. So, I accepted their generous offer.

When I saw their car, I was impressed with its trippy appearance, fully decorated bumper-to-bumper with colorful stickers displaying interesting likenesses and various mantras, everything from "Free Love" to "Beam Me Up, Scotty." These people were on a different level from me, but their kindness was the most important display, and I trusted them for it.

David and Ann's car

AHCH is located downtown on First Street in downtown Albuquerque. As I rode with David and Anna in their hippie mobile, it felt like I lived in a ghost town. The city put homeless people up in hotels and motels around town as a precaution. There were no cars on the roads or the usual people running the streets, selling drugs and their bodies for cash. It was more lonesome and spooky than I'd ever seen it.

When we arrived, I went directly to the reception desk and told them I needed help. I needed to see a therapist now and needed to get some antidepressants to stop the racing thoughts, especially those thoughts of harming myself. I was well on my way to take my life that day. The receptionist suggested I call 911 for help. I tried to explain to the lady who manned the desk behind the plexiglass, "My friends said I could get help there," or something like that. She informed me that the clinic would not treat walk-ins due to the pandemic.

That was it. *Screw this; I tried*. I resolved that God didn't want me to get help; He wanted me to die by taking my own life. I was sure of it. I went to the art therapy room and calmly let David and Anna know I was going to take the city bus or walk home. But that was a lie. I was not going home. I planned on stepping in front of a bus. I explained to them that the suggestion the lady at the desk gave me was to call the police. At the time, there would have been no convincing me to dial that number. I lived in a rough neighborhood. If you were in a police car, you better have robbed someone. Plus, I had warrants for my arrest. I doubted the kind of "help" the police would offer was at all the type I needed.

At that moment, God did for me what I could not do for myself. Christina, the art therapist, stepped in, explaining she was a new staff member. She was appalled at the fact they turned someone away in need of care. Christina didn't know how suicidal I was at that moment, how much I needed someone to care that could really help me. David and Anna had tried, but they aren't licensed mental health workers. Then there was Christina, new and shiny to this place, and knowing what she'd been called to do in her own life: She was there to help people. Christina excused herself and returned a few minutes with an angel named Adam, the head therapist there. He apologized for any miscommunication that may have occurred. He said he would be more than glad to speak with me for as long as I needed.

From that day, for the next couple of years, AHCH was where I received my primary care. I saw my therapists, Ms. Glass and Dr. Green every week without fail, and they helped restore my physical and mental health. The doctors, nurses, techs, receptionists, and therapists are my angels here on earth. God did for me what I could not do for myself. He found me the help I needed to let me live when I was about to die, so I could write this book.

I could have slipped through the cracks that day, gone into the sunset, and killed myself or someone else. God thought differently. Had God not stepped in and gotten me the help when I needed it most, this book would have never seen the light of day. I now teach countless others how to use a God Box. They would have never learned of its power had God not stepped in.

Do you need a miracle like I received? The miracle was a new employee sticking up for someone she'd never met. She didn't realize how urgently I needed help. But God did. And His miracles are more obtainable than you think.

I know why God saved my life that day. I understand why God let the dominoes fall right to get me the help I needed. At the time, God wanted to ensure I was alive to present the gift of how, when, and why to use a God box to show His Power and Love for you. I wonder what God and a God Box will do for you. Scratch that—I don't wonder about it—I'm excited about it. I'm excited for *you*. There's no time to waste!

Let's get started.

The How and What of a God Box

If you're like me, you want to get to the heart of the book. You might be asking yourself, *What must I do to receive God's favor and grace now? Do I need to read the entire book to receive help from a God Box? What's required for me to have peace of mind, prosperity, love, and good fortune? When do I learn the "secret handshake?"* Here's the awesome news: There is no secret to the God Box. It's simple and easy to use.

Still, you really should read the whole book. It might take four hours for a slow reader like me. Break it into four one-hour sessions and enjoy a glass of cool lemonade or a nice cup of steaming chamomile while you learn what God has in store for you. I'll get you started now—no sense in wasting time. I want you to receive God's blessings, favor, and peace of mind just as quickly as you want to.

Are you ready? I sure hope so.

To start, get a box—any box you can label, decorate, or write on. It can be as simple or elaborate as you want. Pop into a craft store or thrift shop, or simply rummage around under your bed. God doesn't care if it's a jewelry box, a shoe box, or an old Amazon box and neither do I.

Once you've picked out your box, write "GOD BOX" in big, bold letters so you can distinguish your God Box from other boxes; we don't want you to mix up your God Box with your recipe box and all the sudden on Thanksgiving Aunt Tillie comes to understand just how big a pain in your life she is. Add religious symbols of your faith if the spirit moves you—though it's not required. Feel free to add whatever inspiration comes to you whether it's a personal mantra or a picture of a blob fish. This is your God Box—keep it as effortless or make it as intricate as you like.

My God Box looks elementary. I received a small wooden box from my wife; flower seeds came in it originally. I use that as my God Box. I wrote "GOD BOX" on all sides to make it perfectly clear what it was and whose it was.

My first God Box

I often make different God Boxes from material I buy from Hobby Lobby. Friends and I get together, and we paint and decorate, calling the gathering a God Box party. For some, getting others involved makes things more fun. But if you think this is a solitary act, that's okay too. I'm really trying to hammer this home: It's up to you! Got it? Good. This is where you will store notes to God.

The key to the box is your own declaration of what it is and what it is for. Set your intention, and take out a piece of paper and a writing utensil. Take a few seconds to think about what you want God to do for you. More money, a spouse, peace of mind, love, or joy? Let your dreams, worries, or needs be your guides. God has no limitations on what He can give you.

Do you want a new Honda SUV or a big house in the country? Do you need a miracle for a friend or family member addicted to drugs, alcohol, porn, or video games? If you don't want to ask for anything for yourself, ask for the well-being of your kids, friends, or extended family. If your religious beliefs prohibit you from requesting money, fame, or love for yourself, put the problems you must face that are out of your control like your grown child's behavior or your brother's trouble with the law. Whatever you feel comfortable putting on that piece of paper, write it down, then put it into your God Box.

And yes, your own God Box can bless others. They do not have to know you put them in your God Box. I told you earlier how wonderful it felt when my brother's problem resolved itself. Paul didn't know I added him to mine. God oversaw the issues and relieved me of the obsession I had no control over. I have done this for many others, and I'm always thrilled watching their lives grow and prosper from a distance.

Put that family member you have love for in your God Box. Add the family member who needs God's special attention for several reasons. Add as many situations or people as needed. I have trouble shutting mine because it is filled with many requests.

Take a look at this list of examples:

- The state of the nation
- The drivers in your city (you think you can control how they drive, but you cannot)
- World hunger
- Climate change
- A friend or family member addicted to drugs

- Job problems (we all have them)
- More money
- A lovely house
- A faster car
- People who talk about you
- The past
- The future

For a long time, I didn't realize the past and the future were out of my control. I didn't know I couldn't control how our president ran our country. I would yell at news anchors as I watched the news, then go to my wife and complain about why those in charge weren't running the United States like I would—with fairness, honesty, and with the people's best interest in my heart. Then I gave the state of the nation to God. I wrote "USA" on a sheet of paper and added it to my God Box.

Then a miracle happened.

Spoiler: The country did not change. I guess that isn't such a big surprise. But what happened was nearly as shocking to me— I did. I changed. I stopped obsessing over what the different political parties were doing. I stopped listening to the gibberish between Democrats and Republicans. I went from watching three news broadcasts daily to one weekly news program. God did for me what I could not do for myself. I no longer need to subject myself to all the ugliness. I now see my country as a beautiful place to live. I feel grateful and blessed to live in the land of the free. And it's all because of my God Box.

As I've mentioned, I want to be in control of everything all the time. Just like the state of the nation, I hated feeling helpless when people I cared about fell sick. A doctor, I am not. I cannot heal people, but God can. I can visit my sick friends and take them food. I can put their names in my God Box, and that helpless feeling fades. God may want to stop their suffering.

He may miraculously heal them for a purpose. I don't pretend to know God's will. How I act and react changes when I put people who are ill or suffer in my God Box. I see God's will in their lives and am more accepting of the outcome. I feel more compassion for those who are sick and those who suffer and rejoice all the more with those who heal. The act of slipping their name into my God Box helps ease my pain for those who pass on to a better place. God is wise and all knowing. Let Him heal you and others in ways you could never imagine.

Be it the nationwide division between people these days or a dear friend's suffering, your God Box will help. Give God problems too big for you and me to manage—the homeless person walking in the street, struggling every day to find food and shelter, or a person you love strung out on fentanyl that you want to save—for both, the answer may be as simple as easier access to public services that could ease their burdens and potentially save their lives. But is it in my or your power to single-handedly change whole systems in our communities when sometimes we're barely able to keep our own lives on the rails? Instead of getting frustrated, give those people to God. Sometimes after putting them in my God Box, God says, "Mark, help them," and then I get busy. Until then, in my God Box they go.

Of course, this isn't carte blanche to do nothing. I still do my part in my community daily. Helping others is a cornerstone of life. Is it required to help others for a God Box to work? No. But expressing your desire to help others might inspire you to act. Then you might discover how good it feels to serve humanity.

Put your needs for God in your God Box. Make many requests but make them meaningful. Think through your submissions and choose carefully what and when you ask. That new job or relationship might require more work than you can handle. Once you've put your slip of paper inside, put the God Box somewhere you can see it. Then let go of whatever you wrote on that paper.

But maybe you still want some clarification on what or how to write these things down. Think of your request like this: Instead of asking for a new job, ask God to take control of your job. Write on a piece of paper, "my job," put it in your God Box, and then let it go. God will get to work doing what He does so well—dispensing grace.

God may give you a new job or employer. He may bless you for doing the same work with a raise in pay. He may reduce your workload, and life becomes less stressful for you. The person causing you pain and discomfort at work might quit, or better yet, becomes an ally instead of a hindrance. If God can do that and more for your job, imagine if you let Him take control of your entire life. He has the universe at His disposal to enrich every aspect of your existence.

If you write down "my job" instead of a "new job," you let God take control of it, and you're no longer in a place where you need to worry about it. Why shouldn't you continue to worry? First of all, worrying about something never changed a darn thing. Second (and more importantly), God knows the best-case scenario. We think we know what is best for us and others. But do we? If God made heaven, earth, and the universe, He knows what is better for me than I do. God knows and can make wiser choices about your life and mine.

Here's an example of God being in control better than you: You drive down the street, going ten miles over the speed limit. You must rush back to work because you and your friend spent a two-hour lunch discussing who wore what at the Oscars (I've done it myself once or twice). You get pulled over by a police officer who gives you a speeding ticket with a hundred-dollar fine. Bad for the pocketbook, but also a miracle from God. Maybe you're thinking, *No way could that be a miracle.* Believe me, the money you had to pay for speeding is divine intervention. It turns out to be the best money you've ever spent. That is God and the God Box doing for you what you cannot see for yourself.

You're probably still thinking, *How can that be a God-given gift?* If you had not been stopped, you might have been hit by a car running a red light at the next intersection and been badly injured. Worse yet, maybe a kid would've darted out from a parked car and you would've tried to stop in time but couldn't. God can give you a speeding ticket just as surely as a police officer and for much the same reason; they both want you to learn to slow down to prevent you from causing an accident the next time. And just so we're clear—God has no quota at the end of the month to incentivize giving tickets—at least, not that I know of, but I've been wrong too many times before to try to guess His motives. We do not always know why God does what He does, but God knows exactly why He does it, and it works.

Do you see my point? First, you should not have been speeding. Second, God and his overall plan are bigger and better than you could ever imagine. God takes control of your world, and when it looks like He might not have your back, He does.

Think about what you want from God and how He can help you. What is it for yourself or others you want God to improve, lighten, or bless you with? You may say, "God knows what I need. Why do I need to tell Him?" For one, God is a gentleman that revels in the art of conversation, even if you don't always hear His side of the banter; for another, when you declare it, you own it. Then there is no question about what you want out of life.

A God Box will strengthen your connection and love for God. It can help others to see His power and love. I love it when God's light shines through me as it demonstrates His glory and genuinely opens the eyes of those who do not believe in a Higher Power. I want to exemplify how God has worked in my life to help others find a Power greater than themselves.

Have you decided what your first slip of paper might contain yet?

Need some more inspiration? It could be your child, spouse, house, school, mental well-being, serenity, love, joy, motivation, overeating, undereating, gambling, addiction, loss, sorrow, anger, sickness, health, meaning of life, more money, the everyday humdrum… The list is endless on what it could be. You just have to make that first decision, and scribble it out.

Remember: The request is between you and God, and no one else.

Make your decision about what you want to turn over to God on paper, write it out, put that paper in the God Box, and read the rest of this book. Put God in charge of things out of your control. Give God the complications in your life that keep you tossing and turning at night.

To recap: Get a box; write on it "God Box" and decorate it as you want; take a sheet of paper and write down your requests for the God of your understanding; fold the paper and put it in the box; close the box and put it somewhere you can see it; let it go.

That last step is crucial. Let it go! Give it to God. Let God get the addicted family member to the realization they have a problem. Have God tell your boss no more micromanaging or unpredictable behavior. God can do for you what would get you in trouble with HR for the use of foul language to a superior. Let God create miracles in your life. God helps in areas of your life you ask him to watch over. I know it to be true, and so will you.

God has you in His arms. He loves you. He wants good things for you and others. Read this book, make your box, and be prepared to experience God's power, strength, and love. Maybe you don't understand how I have the confidence to state that "I know it to be true" and that's okay. A few years ago, I wouldn't have believed those words would ever pass my lips let alone these hands would be typing them in a book, but here I am. Keep reading, and you'll understand better how I got here. I believe that you'll be here by my side too. The one that got me moving was a little old lady. I can't wait to introduce you to her.

My wife's God Box

My Reality

If you're anything like me, then you've been trying your whole life to be a success with no success. It wasn't until I turned my life over to the care of God and my God Box that I even glimpsed significant changes or success. To understand why I'm so passionate about why a God Box works, you must know more about what my life was and how far I've come.

In early 2020, I shot down the very thought of God—let alone ideas on good fortune, favor, or grace. I thought life mistreated me, and that was God's fault. I was a failure at life, love, and happiness, so there was no reason that God would want to bless me with a place to live, a wife to love—anything good, really. It didn't seem possible that my life could take a turn for the better.

Then one day, God sent a little old lady into my life and my entire world changed. Her name was Barbara Shiplet. She was four feet nine inches tall. She weighed eighty pounds soaking wet.

I wasn't always a lying, cheating thief, and Barbara's husband, Gene Shiplet, was my pastor for ten years. I attended Bible study with them every Sunday morning at an Arby's in our town. We met for six or seven years with others like Louie and his family, as well as my friend, Thomas. It was a remarkable gathering of people to learn the word of God.

After some time, the group members went their own way. I stopped paying much attention to God or the Bible. I lost touch with Barbara after Gene died, though I did attend his funeral—hungover on Captain Morgan Spiced Rum and high from smoking meth all night with some woman I knew from rehab. A lot of good rehabs made great connections for me. And who attends funerals sober? They're hard to deal with and it's so much easier when wasted. I told myself, *Gene wouldn't mind. He wouldn't even know. He went to be with the Lord.* That was the last time I saw Barbara until the day she walked back into my life, five years later.

I lived in a fleabag motel and was about to be homeless again. I had no money for food because I spent it on drugs and gambling. My daughter disowned me for good reasons. There was no one to love, and no one loved me. Or so I thought.

Unexpectedly, Louie's wife from the old Bible study sent me a Facebook message. She wrote that Barbara was urgently trying to get ahold of me. She gave me Barbara's number and I called her up. To my surprise, Barbara asked if she could buy me lunch. I quickly agreed; it was an opportunity for a free meal and to ask to borrow some cash (which I would use for drugs and alcohol, of course).

We set a time to meet the next day at an all-you-can-eat buffet. We small-talked briefly as I stuffed my face with roast beef, mac and cheese, sweet and sour pork, and soft tacos. I waited for my chance to ask Barbara for a small loan. I would pay the loan back—or so I told myself, like I always did, even though part of me knew it was a lie. Finally, I worked up the courage. I figured she would pitch me some "turn my life over to the care of God" sermon. She loved to spread God's message. I was ready to muddle through that part—anything it took to secure more cash. But I was far from ready for what Barbara said next.

She looked at me and said, "God told me you needed help, Mark. He said I must find you and ask you to move into my house."

God told her what?! God and I did not speak. I couldn't imagine why I'd be a part of any other discussions He might be having. Why would God want to help me? I now know why and what God's purpose is for me. Back then, I needed clarification. Remember, I lost touch with this woman for five years. I was lost in life and reality. Barbara was off her rocker—it was the only logical explanation.

Why does God care where I sleep when he doesn't care if I eat? Only the day before, I tried panhandling in the snow for food in front of a grocery store. Not one person would even buy me a ham sandwich. I went hungry that night. Yet here I was with Barbara less than twenty-four hours later, overeating until I made myself sick.

At that lunch, I saw her offer as a place to crash; after all, I was on the brink of homelessness. Barbara's only request was no drugs or alcohol in her home. In my head, I figured I could still drink 100-proof peppermint schnapps and shoot up meth in the bathroom, only at a different address. Staying with Barbara until she kicked me out seemed like a good plan—and maybe she'd never catch on to what I was doing outside of her home. After all, she was eighty-five. She wouldn't know if my breath was minty fresh because of mouthwash or hard liquor. I had fooled much wiser people than her. She might never catch me at all.

Today I know God sent me an angel on earth, as he had done at AHCH. She took me in on God's request. Barbara was a divine warrior. Without question, she lived for God and let everyone know it. She said, "God told me you needed help." Answering His call, she invited me into her home. So, I went.

In case you think I wasn't that bad off, I couldn't even bear to walk into Walmart the day I moved in with Barbra. She wanted to buy me some flip-flops so I wouldn't be walking barefoot on the cold white tile at the house.

But I was terrified to go into that store. My paranoia and delusions held me in her little mini-SUV as Barbara went into the store. I cried in her car, ashamed and embarrassed of my behavior—but also relieved that I didn't have to go inside that store.

Two days after I moved in, Barbara left me a note that she was driving herself to the hospital. Her two daughters arrived from out of town and informed me that Barbara would be in the hospital for quite a while. Her daughters, one of whom I had met before, said I was welcome to stay at the house even though Barbara would not be there for months. So, I stayed.

There I was, living in this four-bedroom house with two living areas in a middle-class part of town, complete with the two cutest little dogs that ever loved me. Precious was a little Yorkie who stopped traffic when we walked. She was as dear as any baby you may ever see. I wanted to hold and love her all day. Then there was Perico (Spanish for "Parakeet"), a small, confident, long-haired black terrier that owned the world. He walked purposefully and let the world know he was the man. With my new digs and furry companions, I didn't feel quite as miserable as I was accustomed to.

Obviously, I was still drinking and doing drugs. That had been the plan all along. One day I went for a walk. I got an ice cream cone and walked by a club where men and women were sober. I knew the place well. I sobered up with many of these men and women before. I walked into the non-descript club; there were no signs declaring it as a place where men and women met to get sober, get off drugs, or hold twelve-step meetings for everything from overeating to struggling with a cocaine habit to supporting those that love others with addictions. The only sign on the front of the building was its name: Heights Club.

A man named Big Dave greeted me at the door. He was aptly named as he stood six feet four inches tall. Adding to his height was his brown fedora (reminiscent of Indiana Jones' beloved hat) over his white hair, which matched his white beard. His catchphrase was, "My name is Big Dave, and I've been sober all day." You must have a snappy catchphrase if you're in a twelve-step program. Mine could be catchier, but it works the same: "I know why God saved my life and helped me get clean and sober. It is to help others to do amazing things."

Big Dave told me he was happy to see me. The next words out of his mouth were, "You have a story to tell, and people will listen to you." He gave me a bear hug and instructed me to grab a cup of coffee and take a seat. When Big Dave told you to do something, you did it; he was that kind of guy. So, I poured myself some joe and sat down. God had sent me yet another angel on earth. Only two weeks earlier I'd been crying in Barbara's mini-SUV in a Walmart parking lot, incapable of going inside to pick out a pair of flip-flops.

Why did Big Dave think I could ever tell a story that people would listen to when I could barely explain myself to myself? Why would anyone care what I had to say? I was a mess with one friend in the world (well, three—if you count Precious and Parico). My one (human) friend was a little old lady who was in the hospital near death, and when she'd extended her hand in grace and God, I'd thought she was crazy. But I sat down with my coffee, and here I am today. Sadly, Big Dave passed away two weeks later.

I'll always remember that phrase though, "A story to tell, and people will listen." Today I see God was setting me up for what was coming. I'm no poet. I can't spell. I don't understand the difference between verbs and adverbs. But none of that matters. Now I know what I can do well is tell a good story while describing the truth. Who would ever think I could author a book glorifying the power and love of God? Not me or anyone else I knew at that time. But God and Big Dave did.

To this day, I don't know what drove me to get an ice cream cone and stroll to The Heights Club to get sober, where people with addictions of all sorts meet. I am happy to say since that blistering day, I have not slammed a fifth of Captain Morgan's Spiced Rum or filled a syringe full of methamphetamine. That could have only come from God. Big Dave was right—I have a story to tell, and people will listen.

Three months passed, and finally, my little angel Barbara came home from the hospital. I cooked her meals, and my then-girlfriend (and now-wife), Christie, helped Barbara take baths. Life was good; I was clean and sober. I still dealt with mental health issues, delusions, and depression. Overall, though, life was better than it was.

Barbara was on the mend and things were looking up for me for once. Then out of the blue, Barbara's daughter announced that she wanted to move back in with her mother. I was asked to find my own place. I had lived there for eight months and I didn't want to move out. I was comfortable and I was loved. I also had no choice.

I moved out into a motel paying by the week. Two weeks after I left her home, that lovely lady, my angel on earth, Barbara, passed away, just like Big Dave. I truly miss them both. I know Barbara went to be with God in heaven after fulfilling her commitment to help me. Barbara was called home and I call that amazing grace. I'm sure Big Dave is with everyone who graduated from Alcoholics Anonymous. The only way to graduate from that program is to die sober, just like Big Dave did, and just like he helped others to do.

It's important for you to know about how Barbara and Big Dave intervened in my life because then you can understand that God had a plan for me. God wants me to help others do amazing things, and that amazing thing is to get you what you want and need. To do that, I want you to see there is a Power greater than yourself. You must know that God can do what you cannot do for yourself.

Don't worry if you don't have faith in God. God has faith in you. He wants to see you put in the effort. That is all He asks. Pretend if you must. Fake it 'til you make it. You don't even need to trust in Him. Simply make your God Box. Add your fears and your needs. Then let go of them. Have fun. Enjoy life and let God do the rest. There is a lot we still must learn, but I hope you can find hope in my story as I continue to unravel it so that your life can change for the better, maybe even the best.

All along the most treacherous stones in my path, God affected the way I thought and acted. I just didn't know it for a very long time. Now that I do, I can see how He was there, trying to steer me in a more favorable direction all along.

For example, years before Barbara took me to that buffet or Big Dave welcomed me into The Heights Club, God tried to demonstrate his grace and compassion towards me while working through others—people who I considered my worst enemies. Once again, I was fresh out of jail. My daughter, Monique, had not disowned me at this point. My grandson was four and Monique had recently been in a car wreck. She was seeing a chiropractor for her injuries. She asked if I could go with her and watch my grandson Jack while she was at the appointment. We met at the chiropractor's office. That way, I could take them to lunch afterward.

We met ten minutes before her appointment. I told my daughter I wanted to take Jack two blocks over to Starbucks to get a tasty croissant and a hot caramel macchiato for Jack and me to share while she got her back adjusted. We parted, and Jack and I did our thing. We people-watched. I told him jokes: "Why did the chicken cross the road?" In his cute little voice, he asked, "Why?" I replied, "Cause Kentucky Fried Chicken is next to him, and he wants to get away before Grandpa eats him!" Then I tickled him 'til he nearly peed his pants, squealing with joy.

We finished our fun at the coffee house. It was a cold mid-December day. Snow steadily flurried all around us. We were bundled up with a tasty slice of banana-nut bread for Monique. Her hour was up so Jack and I walked hand in hand back to the chiropractor's office. Traffic was light. I held Jack's hand way too tight, but remember I was fresh out of jail and now on probation. I was lucky my daughter let me have contact with her and Jack—let alone allowing me to take care of him for a whole hour. Nothing was going to happen on my watch.

Here it comes…

Two police cars started shadowing me. I've had my fair share of encounters with the police; I know when they are about to swoop in and arrest me. Thoughts raced through my head: *Do I have a warrant for my arrest that I don't know about? Did someone rob Starbucks, and the police think I'm the culprit? Do the police think I kidnapped Jack?* I didn't know what they were up to, but I was certain I didn't like it.

I took my little grandson in my arms and picked up the pace. If I didn't show up with this child when his mother left her appointment, I would never see either of them again. I shook uncontrollably, not from cold but from fear of never seeing Jack again.

The two squad cars turned on their emergency lights. One cut my path off, its tire going curbside. The other blocked any chance of retreat I had. The officer raced behind me and came to a quick stop, hitting the siren to let me know they meant business. It all happened so fast. Both officers got out of their cars. Jack held tight, and I didn't want to let go. The lead officer asked who the boy was. I explained he was my grandson and that we had just left Starbucks and were heading to meet my daughter half a block away.

The police seemed interested, but not quite convinced. The lead officer asked if it would be okay if he talked with my grandson. I was shocked, but with a crack in my voice, I reluctantly agreed. I set Jack down on his feet, thinking that something bad was about to go down and he may get hurt if he was still in my arms. My life was falling apart in mere seconds.

The lead officer took my Jack by the hand and asked if he had ever seen a police car. *What the hell?* My grandson walked hand in hand with my mortal enemy instead of me. I hated the police. They were pigs—arrogant assholes who harassed good people. In my town, they were known for shooting unarmed men and women. And now here they were taking my grandson away so they could cuff me.

Officer number two approached me and I wavered on full-blown panic's edge. My heart racing, I blurted out something like, "I'm on probation and I'm not supposed to have police contact."

The officer said, "That's okay. It's no big deal."

I thought my probation officer would disagree and that this fiasco was going to be a very big deal—a life-ruining level of big deal. But I was smart enough not to argue the point. I stood there helplessly, waiting for the cuffs to link tight on my wrists. My whole life was slipping away and little Jack was going to bear witness to the exact moment I tumbled down for the last time.

The lead officer opened the front passenger-side door of his car. I started to cry, and the other officer asked if I was okay. The thought came: *Punch this piece of shit, grab Jack, and run for Monique.* But I didn't want to put my grandson through that trauma. I was done for. I tried to accept my fate. The lead officer leaned into the cruiser and pulled out a remote-control car. The officer tried to hand it to Jack, but it was too big for him to hold.

What? What's happening here? I couldn't comprehend anything for a moment.

They told Jack that Santa and his grandpa told them to deliver this. I amended my previous thought as it wasn't nearly profane enough: *What the f***?* The officers explained that they like to give back to the community when they have time. My mortal enemies told my grandson the gift was from me too. I could never have afforded a present like that during those times. My tears ran like a river. I thanked and hugged both of those men. I felt like they were family. If you have ever had contact with police officers when in uniform, a hug is out of the question—but not with these two men on this snowy day. They hugged me right back.

I went home and shared it on Facebook. I didn't care what any of my gangster friends thought. My opinion changed that day about the men and women in blue. I don't care what your opinion is and I'm not trying to change it. I'm just telling my story, like Big Dave told me to—like I said, he was the type of guy that when he told you to do something, you did it. And I'm still doing it. God let me see the love and compassion that police officers can have for others that day. The times that I had police interactions that resulted in me being injured resulted from poor judgment of mine. Today some of my closest friends are police officers and judges.

My opinions on law enforcement would never have changed had God not done for me what I could not do for myself. And what if those honorable police officers had not done that for me? I certainly wouldn't have some of the friends I have today, and honestly, who knows what might have become of me?

What do you need God to do for you that you cannot do for yourself? Is there any enemy or family member you do not want to have contact with? With God's help, all can be restored in an instant. It's time to get over all our hate for one another. Today it's time to be an example of what love looks like. Start anew. Use your God Box for whatever your heart desires. Just be sure to let God give you what you really need.

What Can You Get with a God Box?

One of the first things to do is find out why you need a God Box. What do you want or need from your life? Is it property and prestige that eludes you? Are you tired of living in the same old house with worn-out carpet and bumble-bee-yellow wallpaper? Is your kitchen outdated, and would you like a new one? Is your car in need of repair, and you're desperate for the money to fix it? Are people the problem in your life that need adjustments?

Better yet, are you the problem and you just can't seem to find the strength or wisdom needed to change your life? Are you tired of a broken system that never seems to work for you? What is out of your control that needs God's attention?

Maybe you're tired of puppy love—and I'm not talking about when you come home, and that lovable four-legged sweetheart bounds happily to greet you with kisses and little grunts. That's wonderful! But it's hard to share a nacho platter with all the fixings with your puppy (the cleanup alone should be enough to steer clear of that idea). Puppies are fun, and they love you with all the might of their tiny hearts. That love, however, differs from falling in love and experiencing love with another human. We all seek love that kind of love. It's essential to most everyone's lives to feel complete, and yet, it can be so dang hard to find. Your God Box can help you find lasting, meaningful relationships. Is that what you're looking for?

Perhaps it's none of these things. Only you know what it takes to make your life feel more complete. I can guess all day, but everyone's different.

It's time to ask yourself what you want from a God Box. If you're like me, you might ask for a new pair of Nikes and a boat; I want a houseboat so badly I can practically feel the rock of the water beneath me right now. So, I added that into my God Box. I wrote "houseboat" on a piece of paper and put that paper inside, and when God feels the time is right—Lake Mead, here I come! Not that I want to give you the impression that it's always easy and quick. Sometimes it is; sometimes, it isn't. Remember, this is on God's time. He's the Wise One.

I'll add a piece of paper in my God Box with my request for an Xbox, and boom—my wife will buy it for my birthday. Awesome as that is… Honey, I don't want an Xbox for my birthday. Now the boat, on the other hand, I'll happily take.

This isn't about me, though. I have what I want and need. This is about you and your desires or necessities. Maybe you need some help figuring out. Maybe you're at a point where the list seems endless, and you need a hand narrowing it down. I have a few suggestions to get you started.

Car: Make it a nice one if you're going to ask (might as well make it count). I know what I said earlier—don't be specific. But I just can't help myself! I want a fast and fancy one.

Love: This is a big one for all of us. I'm married, and I still have love in my God Box. I want to be a more loving person. I want friends and family to love me and themselves. I want love for all of humanity. God put us in this world to love. Before I added love to my God Box, I was ugly. I hated people who saw life differently than me. Today I love people with different ideas and concepts.

I love to hear about others' journeys, what it's taken to get them from point A to point B. I am the love I love to see in the world. Do you need love in your life? Ask for it. Then you'll see love from the One who originated the concept.

House: Tired of your apartment? Do noisy neighbors keep you up all night? Ask God and your God Box for a home.

Fun trinkets: Perhaps you're just not having the fun you want to in life and an RV, jet ski, or a boat (like me) would lift your spirits and put the smile back on your face. I know I'm having fun with these requests. God can and will give you material goodies. God didn't put us on this earth to be miserable, and it's very hard to have a terrible time on a jet ski.

A miracle: I know some of you need a miracle healing for you or others. Put that diagnosis in your God Box for now and ask God for His divine help. I'm not going to pretend you will get one. I don't want to give anyone false hope. I do know that God can heal the sick. Blessings can come spontaneously. That blessing may fall on you or someone you care about if you ask. If it doesn't, what I've learned is that if it is their time to pass from this world, I'm more at ease with the pain of losing a loved one. Also, and to my surprise, when I add that terminally ill person to my God Box, I've seen their response to death change. They seem to make peace with it, which not only helps them but those left to grieve.

Addiction: Are you or someone you know suffering from alcohol, drug, porn, or shopping addictions? The list of addictions could go on for pages, so I'm not going to attempt to name them all here, but you get my drift. Do you need God to help you or that loved one break that addiction ruining lives? God and a God Box can and will heal those suffering. Of course, the addict must want to get well. God cannot heal someone if they want to stay sick. Check that—God corrected me and said, "He can do anything He pleases." Add the person or persons with an addiction that needs God's hand in their recovery. He said He would do it, and I believe Him.

Money: Who couldn't use more money? I know I certainly can. I could buy new furniture for the house. The new car I hope to get will need gas, and the insurance on a Land Rover will be outrageous. I'll need money for those payments. I don't have a new Land Rover yet; you better believe it's going in my God Box. My dream trip is to take my entire family to Disney Land with the money God and my Box will bring me. I'll kick back and eat a churro while the kids risk their lives on The Twilight Zone Tower of Terror. I have books to write (and churros to munch). The point is we could all use a little money. Write "money" on paper and add it to your God Box. Better yet, add a dollar bill to your God Box. God will provide.

The next three I must include. Well, I don't *have* to, but I'll get the look from the wife if I don't. Christie's the one who started me on this journey. She, without question, would want me to add the following suggestions.

Serenity: I'll have all kinds of serenity on the Toy Story Mania ride at Disney! You can too! But I know that's not what my sweet wife wants me to talk about (really, honey, I know). She means finding serenity when life throws a curve ball or in the humdrum of everyday life. My wife and I include the word "serenity" in our God Box. You don't have to go to any Magical Kingdom to have serenity and peace (though surely that can't hurt). With the God Box, I have learned to accept where I am today. If you want serenity, write the words down on paper and be prepared to be amazed. Next year—Splash Mountain, here I come! (Sorry, honey, I can't help myself.)

Acceptance of others: Do I have to? I hate the way some people act, but I must accept it. According to the experts, I do. Control of others is out of my control. The best I can manage is to be my best example to others. God and my God Box have taught me to look at others causing chaos in the world as sick people, as I once was. I don't have to like their behaviors; I don't have to invite them to dinner and explain why I think they're wrong. What I do is add the words "behavior of others" then give them to God to do with them as He sees fit.

Outcomes: God is in control; I cannot control my life to the extent I want to (another difficult thing to accept). I proved how out of control my life could get with drugs and alcohol. God told me to do the work regarding my sobriety and leave the outcome to him. If I work on this book every day for two years, that still doesn't mean it will make it to print. Do you know who can control these things? God can. I put in the work and leave the results up to Him. This book, *The Beauty of a God Box,* goes inside my Box. Is that a conundrum? Maybe, but because of Him and my Box, I can accept it. Let God worry about your life's little and big outcomes.

Those three are very important; Christie is sharp and generally, I heed her advice. I recommend you do the same. But I'm me, so I had to save one of my favorite requests for last.

Nifty things: Why nifty? It sounds cool, plus it's those items that you'd never ask for yourself or think you want or need. For you, maybe it's some Beats headphones, a swimming pool, or a trip to Spain. A nifty thing I received might be quite simple to others, but to me, it was just that—nifty. Please, allow me to digress. (Wait—why am I asking for permission? It's my book!) Enjoy my digression. (Much better.)

I was at a gathering of two hundred like-minded friends. We were at a bar where a film production company was promoting all aspects of the film industry in New Mexico. There was a raffle and others bought ten or twenty tickets. I bought one. They had fantastic prizes like acting classes and studio time, but what caught my eye was the smallest one up for grabs, a coffee mug.

I saw that coffee mug and knew I had to have it. Meow Wolf, an immersive art adventure installation with over seventy rooms in Sante Fe, donated it. I couldn't afford to take my wife there as I was on disability (my monthly income was $1300 a month, and added to my wife's small income, we could still barely afford a monthly movie visit). But I could win a mug, dang it.

When they announced the mug would be drawn next, I was enthusiastic, to say the least. I jumped up and down, begging God to let me win the mug. I wanted something to remember this awesome event. One of the ladies, in her colored hair and flamboyant black and white dress with matching heels, grabbed my attention from the bar. She asked my name and I told her. She said something like, "Good luck. I hope you win. I haven't seen anyone this excited to win any of the prizes."

They called the winning number and it was mine. I won!

I walked up there and received my nifty mug. When I add hot water to it, trees appear all around the outside and well, I think it's too cool for school. But that isn't the coolest part of the story. The lady who wished me luck winning the mug is the social and community manager at Meow Wolf, Shanny Schmidt. Shanny gave me free tickets to the niftiest art experience. The tickets were not a part of the prize—they weren't tucked into the mug or anything like that. She simply saw how excited I was to win, and she gave them to me. God is good!

My wife and I would never have been able to go without help. We made a day out of it that we'll never forget. We ate delicious tacos at Thomasite's in Santa Fe (and I overindulged in salsa and chips—I couldn't help from devouring that salsa and I highly recommend you do the same 'cause it's the *best*) after spending hours at Meow Wolf, exploring its many rooms and marveling at its design (it really is a one-of-a-kind experience, but so very hard to describe). It's a day I'll never forget, centered around an opportunity to experience something I wish all people could. Ask for nifty things and see what God has for you out of the ordinary.

Digression over (for now). Now it's pen to paper time.

Take a piece of paper and write down the things you want God to start working on in your life right now. Ask that your wants and needs be met, whatever they might be for you.

Maybe you're thinking that the act of writing something down and tucking it into a box is no different than a prayer. Or maybe you're thinking that good things happen all the time to other people and they don't use a God Box. Maybe you're thinking about eating too many chips and salsa after a wonderful day at Meow Wolf. No matter what you're thinking, I want you to know that I understand good things come to people with no faith, no God, and no God Box.

And I wouldn't want it any other way.

That's because I was a person without those things too, but now I understand He was working for me even when (at best) I was irate with Him. As much trouble as I've had and caused in my life, God was always there. The same is true for you, for all of us. Maybe you think that you've done too many terrible things for God to care about you, but He does. I've done terrible things and my relationship with God is stronger than ever. I have a loving wife, a home, and car. A few years ago, I didn't think I deserved those things either. But here I am.

And you ain't heard nothing yet.

Jot down your requests and seek God's blessings

Control

We need to examine the situations we think we have control over but do not. The conditions that keep us up at night are usually ones where there's no simple solution, but the hard truth is often that for us, there's no solution we can provide at all. I had to learn the hard way that I was not in control of anything except for how I reacted to life.

There are plenty of websites out there that will give you lists of things outside of your control, but here are a few that particularly irk me:

- The past
- The future
- Actions of others
- Dealing with life on life's terms
- Politics
- How others react and/or feel
- Changes (whether they're expected or not)
- Weather

The list could go on and on, but let's look at a few off the top with real-world applications.

The past: If your spouse ran off with their coworker and they are now married, that is certainly out of your control. There is nothing you can do to change any occurrence in the past. It is not humanly possible. For you, a God Box will let the past be what it is—the past. The hurt and pain you feel will subside when you use your God Box.

The future: You have no clue what's in store for you tomorrow or ten minutes from now. For all you know, you get a phone call from the ER while you read this book. They inform you that your mother slipped in the shower and has broken a hip. Now your life has changed drastically. You had no clue that was coming! But who would? That's in the future, and no matter how hard you try, you cannot predict what's going to happen. A God Box will not prophesize for you. It will teach you to live in the present, the here and now. There will be no more worry about the future.

The next phone call you get could be from the company at which you applied for a job. They're calling to let you know you got the gig. Ten minutes from now, you may get a Facebook message from a lost love wanting to reconnect. Tomorrow, you could learn you picked all the winning numbers for the giant jackpot lottery. You have no clue what the future holds. If you add the word future to your God Box, guess who is now in control of it? That's right! The answer to worrying about the future is God (gold stars to all you who've been paying attention and got it right).

Actions of others: One day, my wife and I watched a spooky movie in bed. I love good scares. I was holding a pillow close to me. My wife was smiling (she's not a big chicken like me). We focused on watching the movie until, out of the blue, on our street, a person or persons shot a semi-automatic weapon for no reason. After ducking for cover, we got up and went outside. No bullet holes punched in our house or the neighbors'. Talk about having no control over the action of others!

I was mad and wanted to punish someone. I spent the rest of the night wondering who or why someone would do that. My wife put it in her God Box and let God have it. (How does she do that?) I worried while she enjoyed the rest of the movie. Like I told you from the beginning, this is one I have trouble with, so follow Christie's example. I know I do, and it's getting better all the time, even though I need to keep working on it. Remember, we're on God's time.

Dealing with life on life's terms: Can you control if a car runs a stop sign and T-bones you? Nope, no way to stop that from happening. You must deal with it. The best way to deal with the hand you're dealt is to give it to God and your God Box. I don't like the fact that the judicial system is a joke, but it is a circumstance out of my control. If I do not like it, I should avoid it.

What circumstance is out of your control? Do you not like the way your mother-in-law behaves? Do you not like the man or woman your sister is about to marry? As much as you would like to think those and other circumstances are in your control, they're not. Put your mother-in-law's name in your God Box and see how God will change her attitude and how you react to her comments. It really is that easy.

Politics: This can be a big one for some people. I know in the past, it was for me. I dislike the way the country is run. Policymakers should be running this country differently. I don't care if we're talking about the president of the United States, Congress, or the mayor of my town. They suck. I want a key to the city someday so Mr. Mayor I was talking about the other guy. Sure, I can vote for those who could do a better job in office, but once they're in, what they do and the policies they make are out of my control. I let God and my God Box handle all that, and once I did, it made all the difference in my life.

Add the opposite political party that goes against your wishes into your God Box. Maybe God will change the way they think and act. Better yet, I assure you it will change *you* for the better. You don't have to even mean it. Showing God that you are willing to write it down and give it to Him is enough. Get ready to enjoy life without worrying if your taxes are going to the poor or the rich. God is in control. It will go where God wants it to go.

Believe it or not, you control your thoughts and actions. Little else. You can control how you react to certain situations and what you think about what's happening in the world around you. If you dislike how someone behaves, can you change what they're doing? Yes, if you want to get violent and go to jail—you can (though I don't recommend it). What you can do is make them see life from your perspective. You can be an excellent example of what or how you think they should conduct themselves. Sorry to inform you that even your kids' actions and thoughts are out of your control, but it's the truth.

Do you know who can change the way people think and act? God can. God did it for me. I thought it was okay to steal from others. Shoplifting was a daily way of living. The judge, the police, what my mom thought or tried to do—none of it stopped me. It was not until God stepped in and changed my life. With my drug addiction, I didn't have control over myself. I wanted to stop stealing many times. I wanted to stop doing drugs and drinking. I wanted to be a better son, father, and man. But I couldn't. I could not control my drug addiction. I tried to limit my daily use to no avail. I could not do it. I had to let go and give it to God to handle. God did his magic on me, and I stopped doing the things that were causing me and others harm, big and small, including shoplifting.

God and a God Box have taken the situations out of my control and fixed them. Yeah, God not only meets my needs and wants—He also gives me peace of mind. I wanted to bring up shoplifting because lots of people have done it, even if only as kids. Most people seem to remember sneaking a candy bar or something else small at some point, and most people agree it was a dumb thing to do. But that's small potatoes stuff. I've done much worse, and I still got to come back into His arms and still receive His gifts.

Many examples I give in this book have to do with my criminal past, but what can I say? It was a big part of my life. It is also a great example of God turning my life around when He and I didn't have an excellent relationship, and as much as I sought control, everything was spinning out in my life.

The last time I was in jail, I was in a peculiar position. I had already pleaded guilty to three felonies and was out on drug court. If you're unfamiliar with drug court, it's when you're given a drug court officer that keeps track of you with check-ins and weekly drug tests, among other things. My drug court officer was Anthony Rodolfo. He expected a lot from me but was also an understanding, fair man. Anthony had me meet with a counselor every week, attend daily AA meetings, and called me often to make sure I was doing all I needed to do. I had to talk with a judge monthly about my progress, attend classes, and even do a little community service here and there. Overall, if I followed Anthony's direction, it would take about a year to complete. Anthony's job is not a glamorous position, but he worked hard for me. I can't thank him enough for all the help he offered and provided. We are still friends to this day, and I even spent a Thanksgiving with him and his family. God is good.

But I was not.

After six months in drug court, I absconded. I stopped taking drug tests. I no longer made my scheduled appointments with Anthony.

While on the run, I committed more crimes, including forging and cashing checks totaling about five thousand dollars at a casino. After that venture, I was well known to the police and had been on the news. While I tried to lay low, a friend of mine was driving me somewhere when police lights and sirens sparked up behind us. I asked, "Did you run a light or something?" but she told me she hadn't. My heart sank. Suddenly, three unmarked cars boxed us in. Officers leapt from the vehicles, guns drawn. You see, they'd been told I was carrying a gun. I was considered armed and dangerous, even though I was no Jesse James. I was just a plain ole fraud.

They'd also been informed that there was no way I'd go back to jail peacefully. As far as I was concerned, I'd much rather be dead than spend another minute in a cell. Right now, just thinking about being back inside, brings tears to my eyes. I'm no tough gangster either. And back then, I was a dumb man who'd lost his way, doing dumber things to get the drugs that kept me lost. All I could think as I looked down the barrels of their guns was, *They're gonna have to kill me to get me out of this car.*

The girl next to me screamed, "Don't shoot! Don't shoot!" She held up her hands, pleading for her own life as she looked down those same barrels.

I screamed beside her, "Shoot me or I'm going to kill you!" I stared at the plain-clothes cop standing dead-center in front of me, with nothing to take cover behind. As he commanded me to show him my hands, I defied him, shouting death threats instead. I kept my hands tucked into my hoodie's pockets, waiting for him to pull his trigger. This was the only way I could think of to control my fate. I was going to go out on my terms, and no one was ever going to shove me into a cell again.

The next few seconds played out in slow-motion. I moved like I was getting ready to pull my weapon out of the hoodie, watching that officer right in front of me steeling himself to pull his trigger. He was going to kill me and justifiably. At the time, Albuquerque Police Department was under federal investigation for shooting and killing people without defense. I wanted to make sure this wasn't going to be one of those cases.

I went to draw out from my hoodie completely with the intent of being shot and killed. Then, an act of God occurred. The passenger window's glass exploded by my head. I was hit. I fell to the side, and the next thing I remember is being dragged out through the window. It's a bit of a blur, but then I was on the ground and the cops reached for my weapon.

One of the undercover cops shouted, "Are you f***ing kidding me?!" He was mad as hell as he held up what he'd pulled from me, showing the other officers—my phone.

I told you, I'm no Jesse James.

I had a plan to die by way of suicide-by-cop. But I hate violence. I wasn't going to shoot anyone. I just wanted someone else to shoot me.

I failed there too. The glass didn't shatter because of a bullet, but a baton (I think—as I said, it's a bit blurry). I was in pain and bleeding from the shards cutting me, not from being shot.

My mother had the chance to talk with those officers later, and in particular the one I locked eyes with, the one that had no cover if I really had possessed a gun and an intent to fire. She thanked him up and down for not killing her son, for showing restraint with his weapon. He told her the oddest thing.

He said, "Something in my spirit told me he didn't have a gun." He was right. But that's a heck of a risk to take when someone's screaming that they'll shoot you.

To add insult to injury, the woman driving me that night had turned me in when she'd been busted for a drug deal earlier. I know that my life story sounds like a bad movie. I wish there were at least exciting cameos from unexpected celebrities, but not in this act.

After I went to the hospital to get glass removed from my flesh, I sat in county jail, the very place I was so desperate to avoid. My public defender lawyer suggested I plead incompetent to stand trial. He looked at me as crazy. To this day, I have no clue why he thought I was crazy. I was sane at the time (in case you have your doubts too—not that I blame you). The public defender wanted me to see a trained doctor to decide if I could stand trial. It was on. I knew the wait to see a doctor would be months, though I had no clue it would take over a year. So, I sat in jail and did my homework for the exam.

The whole time I waited, I asked every common and not-so-common criminal I was incarcerated with if they knew what questions were on the test. I had a whole year to prepare, so I figured I'd better study up. I also had one brother who had schizophrenia and another who suffered from mental and emotional trauma that left him with issues. I could fake insanity if I needed to, and I couldn't imagine a time I'd need to more.

I knew I could fake it, and I did. After what seemed like forever, I saw the doctor, and when he finally gave his final report, it said I was crazy. I beat the system! Hooray!

I thought I would be home soon, but I was soon disappointed. Although suitable for the new charges I picked up while on drug court, it was bad news for the original charges. The diagnosis could not be used in the first case. I was in limbo. My public defender didn't know what to do with me; months passed with nothing. Finally, one day my lawyer came to see me, only to say he could not represent me. He felt he was unqualified to handle my case, so he shuffled my case off to Mr. Works. I had been in jail for over six hundred days and was about to get a new public defender who had to start from scratch.

Kill me. Kill me now, is all I could think. I was no murderer. My crimes weren't violent or sexual. I made some fake IDs and cashed in a few stolen checks. Yes, I had eight previous felony convictions—but for similar crimes, like identity theft. Stockbrokers and bankers steal millions of dollars and spend less than six hundred days in federal prison, let alone county hell. I hadn't even been sentenced. And after all those days, suddenly I've got a new lawyer. I've rarely felt so helpless, so unable to control my own destiny.

After seven hundred days in county jail, my new lawyer, Mr. Works, came to jail to meet me. I was called from my cell, and when I walked in, I saw this nerd with glasses who looked smart enough but was no Johnny Cochran. He politely stood up and introduced himself.

Then he asked me my name. I answered, "Mark." He asked me about my birthday and I told him it was in March. Finally, he asked me what day it was and I replied, "It's Tuesday."

The following words out of Mr. Works' mouth floored me: "You are not crazy. Judge Sanchez will never believe you are incompetent." I started to tell him I could fake it. And he shut me down quickly, "Don't tell me—I don't want to know."

He explained the complicated situation I was in. Then he dropped the bomb on me. He could get me fifteen years in prison with good time. That would mean I would be out in seven and a half years with good behavior. My mind raced with fear. "No way," I said. "I can't do it. I will take my life. I'll go to my cell right now and hang myself."

Then God stepped in.

Mr. Works told me about a new program the courts had started. In fact, he was the one who helped bring it together. I don't know how much influence he had on forming the group, but he was convinced he could sway the rest of the panel to accept me into the program. He still had to convince the judge and district attorney to go for it, and he admitted it was a long shot. I don't know whether Mr. Works and I believe in the same God or not—for all I know, he's an atheist— but as I recall, he said, "If you believe in prayer, you better pray." I took his advice.

Those prayers worked. I was accepted into the mental health court. Mental health court was a lot like drug court, only longer and more intense, and with loads more therapy. I had a long haul before me: I had to complete two years of mental health court with no violations, a year of house arrest, and years of probation. If I did not complete the terms of my plea deal, I would have to go to prison for twenty-eight years. And that hard time was set in stone. No doubt about it. There would be nothing anyone would be able to do for me. No appeals to file. No excuse for me being mentally incompetent to help in my own defense. No excuses if I failed.

I am happy to report that I did it. I made it and have not returned to jail since that day. Well, since we're being completely honest, there was one time when I was in mental health court and the supervisor lied to the judge about how I failed a drug test. She wanted me to go to prison. But don't worry—she got hers, and she was fired.

What does this have to do with you? Everything. You have to see how God worked for me throughout my life so I could bring you this remarkable power of God and a God Box. I want to give hope to all of you through the story of my life that God is in control.

When we think, we know life's how, where, and when—that's an illusion. God has a plan for us. What that plan is? I do not know. God does. God wants you to enjoy a life full of bountiful spiritual gifts. Not only peace of mind, but tangible gifts to enjoy and cherish. And some foolish things that you can have fun with.

God will not deliver you from hell to have you broke and unsatisfied with life.

But enough about that, I want you to have your heart's desires, the fun stuff, exciting things. I want you to get material possessions with your God Box—but I also want you to feel relief from the frustration of things outside of your control. I'm not sitting in prison right now not because I should have been in control, but because I wasn't, and God sent many people to help set me on a better, healthier path. I don't expect you to be as bad off as I was, though maybe you are. Whether you're worried terrible rain will ruin your romantic weekend away or you're afraid your medication isn't working as well as it used to—add those things to your God Box. I want you to see the power God will bring to your life with one simple box. But first, we better do a little work.

Pen to paper time!

Write down the things that are out of your control in your life. Write them down on paper and add those to your God Box. Nothing more and nothing less to do. Write down as many things as you want. Not the cool stuff, not the material goodies, but scribble down the things out of your control. When God blesses you with serenity or a bag of money, you let people know a God Box worked for you. Trust me, there's plenty of good stuff to go around.

One of the fancier God Boxes

Rainbows and Unicorns

As optimistic as I want to be in this book, I also have no intention of lying to you. No matter how good life can get, the truth is that every day's not going to be filled with the delightful magic of rainbows and unicorns. We need to learn to deal with life on life's terms; otherwise, we'll be miserable. Some of us have challenging situations to handle from the day we're born. Some (like me) have created a difficult life for themselves. But here's the good news—there are tools we can use to change our lives! The possibilities are endless with God, and the God Box is a tool that gives us access to God's grace.

Will the God Box help you get more money, a different house, or a better job? Absolutely, if that's what the God of your understanding wants and has in store for you. God wants us to have peace, love, and serenity. God wants us to prosper. The only restriction is that we do not interfere with others' peace, tranquility, or well-being.

And maybe there's what some may call a catch, others, perhaps, karma— but either way I think you could see it coming.

We've got to look out for others too.

I know, I know—I've been building up your dreams of all that a God Box might do for you. But surely your dreams aren't all solo adventures! We've got to share in the good stuff, just like back in kindergarten. For example, if you wrote down "better job" and tucked it into your God Box, there's a lot you can do when you get it, whether it's a promotion or a whole new career. In fact, a better job is the best chance for the most good for everyone. That extra money coming your way? God expects you to spread that around a little. You don't have to go find an unhomed person living in a tent without shoes and give them every extra cent, though. As wonderful a deed as that might be, God doesn't expect you to personally turn strangers' lives around—remember, He wants you to be happy too. It's okay to think big, but it's okay to think small too. Maybe God wants you to give to your church or a single mother striving to make ends meet. Perhaps, your work schedule is less hectic and instead you donate some of your time to cleaning up a park or helping at a food bank. Or it could be simpler and closer, like helping out your daughter on a car payment so she has safe transportation. These smaller acts can have gigantic impact on individuals in your community and family.

If your slip of paper just said, "money," be sure to ask God, "Where do you want me to donate the money you have waiting for me now that I use a God Box? How much should I give?" I know God wants me to donate twelve percent of book profits to reputable charities. I think I can negotiate it down to ten… On second thought, I better stick to twelve.

A quick aside here—I want to make it clear that God speaks to me. Sometimes, it's an intuitive thought. But because I've worked on my relationship with Him, I now hear his voice. I ask, and He answers. I know that makes me sound crazy—in fact, I thought I might be losing my mind. But I talked with my therapist about God's voice and she assured me that I'm not. I didn't really need her to tell me that, but I figured it didn't hurt to double-check. I don't hear voices that aren't real; I hear God's voice. Let me tell you, it's like nothing I've ever experienced in my life. After being reassured that my mind was still sound, I now relish that audible voice in my head, guiding and helping me on big and little things. I thought you should know that's where I'm at with my relationship with God and what I mean when I say He told me something.

Now that we've clarified that—back to my point about helping others.

A God Box will always work to help you deal with life on life's terms. Everything could be going great, and then it isn't—that's because life is complicated, and we have to accept things for what they are. For instance, if your soulmate asked for a divorce but isn't clear as to why it's necessary, that would be confusing and painful. You also know that you can't browbeat someone into staying married to you—that isn't healthy for either of you. Adding "divorce" to your God Box can change the outcome. Maybe now your partner opens up to you and together you can work on problems to improve your marriage. Maybe God sends you the true love of your life and now you recognize that you'd be happier out of the marriage too. Better yet, you find peace alone and explore a new world you never knew existed now that you have freedom to do so. Using a God Box and letting God do the work is much better than sitting around and feeling sorry for yourself. It helps us accept those people and things beyond our control and live the lives we've always wanted to live—whether or not we knew it was what we wanted. He knows what's best for us. Let God and a God Box turn a negative into a positive.

The beauty of giving your life over to God via the God Box is it is now out of your hands, off your shoulders, and no longer spinning gears in your head. Now it is up to God to send the right people to help you. It is up to God to create miracles to heal and help guide your loved ones in the right direction.

If you don't think blessings, miracles, or favors happen, I *know* they do. I see the proof in my life and the lives around me. I've witnessed countless others turn their will and care over to God, drastically changing their lives. They have mastered turning their addictions, families, and friends to God. The God Box is a tangible aid to help you achieve this mastery.

My ex-mother-in-law, Rose, is a prime example of what we should strive for when we turn our lives over to the care of the God of our understanding. She was diagnosed with a rare bone disease. It showed up on the x-rays that her toes would have to be amputated. That was just for starters. The prognosis was dire for her. She was in the hospital, and the family did not think she would survive this.

But Rose is one lady who believes in her Higher Power. She has loved God through good times and bad. Even with her grim prognosis, she never stopped loving or trusting God. She didn't use a God Box because Rose never needed the physical act of putting those worries, wants, and needs into a box. Turning her life over to the care of God came naturally. She did it with her marriage, kids, and her life. Rose instinctively turned to God and declared her need and trust with mind, body, and soul.

Rose was never negative about her situation. She prayed, asked God to take it away, and then let it go. One day the x-ray showed the bone disease and they would have to start by cutting off her foot. Then who knows what would be next. God didn't see it that way the next day she was healed. The tumor, disease was gone! Her doctors couldn't explain how or why she was restored to health. Today, she is still free of any illness. That, my friends, is God doing for us what we—nor any doctor, friend, family member, man, or woman—could not do for us or ourselves. For her part, Rose shares her story with anyone willing to listen. She is a ray of hope and light in many lives, and continues to spread His message as a living miracle.

Will God bring you a miracle? I believe so. But I am not God; I do not understand why God does what he does. When I trust in God, I give it to Him to handle, and it always turns out better than I could have done or even imagined. Even when we have lost, be patient, and God will show us we have won.

Life is not always easy. I get that. Not everyone can be granted a healing miracle like Rose. Trust me, I know.

The second most challenging day of my life was when my brother Chris passed away.

I cried for my loss and rejoiced in the good times I shared with him. I was and am still thankful to God that Chris is no longer suffering. The day he died, my wife and our friends cried, laughed, and shared fond memories of his life. To this day, I feel honored to have a brother who was so gentle and kind.

I would love for you to have met him.

I could be mad at God for taking him too soon, for not giving Chris the healing miracle that He bestowed upon Rose. Instead, I try to the best of my ability to look for good in situations and not wallow in my selfish feelings. Yes, I want him here with me. However, Chris chose to stop chemo; he was tired of fighting his illness.

His passing is what he wanted, and I honor him for that decision. I could sulk and complain, but I do not let my mind dwell on negative thoughts about his passing. My God and my God Box help me to keep my thoughts and perceptions positive in every situation.

One of the many times I got out of jail, my mom, Bea Ann, picked me up from release. I got in the car with her, but instead of going straight to her house, I asked her if she would drop me off at an Alcoholics Anonymous meeting. It was close to four-thirty in the afternoon, and I knew there was a meeting at that time.

Many of my friends took part in this group and I wanted to start my sobriety over again. My mom laughed at me and said, "Look at you—those are the clothes you wore when you were arrested six months ago. At least let me take you to Walmart and buy you a pair of twenty dollars shoes and some gym shorts." But I refused the offer.

No, that isn't exactly right. Something overwhelmed me. I wanted to go to this group, but suddenly, I *needed* to go to this exact meeting. It was probably because I wanted to see my ex-girlfriend at the time. She was in recovery, and I heard through the grapevine that she had moved on while I sat in a cell. She wasted no time moving on for good reasons. I don't blame her. Who wants to date some fool who was on the news for fraud and forgery?

I thanked my mom for the offer but wanted to get to the group and share my experience. I wanted to talk about finding strength and my hope that crime does not pay. Drinking and drug addiction was the way I found the courage to commit crimes. I was working on finding a new source of courage every time I got sober. I just had to get to the meeting and talk about what I'd been going through.

My mom dropped me off and said she would pick me up after the meeting. I walked into the room that held sixty people at best. When I arrived, there were only around twenty people there; a few I knew, but most I did not. The girl I was dating before I was arrested, walked up to me, kissed me on the cheek, and wished me well on my journey. That was after she laughed at me. The clothes I wore looked atrocious. I had on dress pants that were wrinkled from waist to ankle, a button-up shirt missing a button, and black dress shoes scuffed and dirty from the scuffle I had with the police.

My friend, Jim (not his real name), came in. He's a six-foot tall, good-looking man I have known for years. By no means is he rich. As he walked towards me, I met him halfway, and he greeted me with a warm hug, welcoming me back. He, like my ex, started laughing. He said, "What the hell? Did you come straight from jail?"

I laughed with him and gave him the gist, "It wouldn't have mattered if I went home. All I own is long gone. The motel I stayed at surely threw out my stuff months ago."

At that declaration, Jim looked me up and down, placed his size-thirteen shoe next to mine, and ordered me to follow him. We walked outside to his car. He popped open the trunk, and I saw ten pairs of Nike shoes (looking brand new), gym shorts with the Nike swish up and down, and shirts with Michael Jordan stretched out, ready to slam dunk a ball. Jim said, "Take your pick."

I couldn't believe it. "What? I can have a shirt?"

He laughed, took a pair of shoes, and told me to try them out and see how they felt. The black and gold high tops fit like gloves on my feet. He pulled out some green and grey shorts, held them up to me, and said, "These should fit you." If not, they had drawstrings. He finally had me try on one of the shirts to see if it was the right size. Like the fabled Goldilocks, I found it was just right, like it was meant for me.

His generosity in giving me those gym shorts, shirts, and shoes shocked me. Who does that? God and people like Jim, that's who. The fun didn't stop there.

That man gave me four pairs of shoes and four pairs of shorts, each with a matching shirt. I still own the green pair of shorts and a couple of shirts he gave me over ten years ago.

What was my friend Jim doing with all this gear in his trunk? An hour before, he went to a thrift store to sell some of his slightly used clothes. He needed money for rent, and the amount they offered him was decent but less than what he needed. He explained that God had told him not to take the money. God had a more important purpose for the clothes. I was that important purpose. I said it once and I'll keep saying it: God is good. When my mom picked me up from that meeting, she was amazed I was in all new clothes. Well, new to me, which was still pretty impressive compared to what I was wearing when she dropped me off.

I'm happy to report Jim was blessed too; one of our mutual friends loaned him the money he needed and waited graciously for repayment until Jim's financial issues were resolved. God did that for me, but I think he did it for me to show you His power and that it's easy to trust in God. My point is: You don't always have to ask to receive his gifts.

But asking makes it easier.

My other point is that we should ask for others, and we should use our gifts to help others when we can. Rose lived and Chris died; God had a plan in mind for both of them. I insisted on going to that meeting in my disheveled state, but God and Jim stepped in to clothe and shoe me. A little faith in Him, or even just in one another, goes a long way. Your God Box should be used as a conduit between you and Him, but also as a connection to others.

With His gifts in your life, there's no reason not to spread the good stuff around. It's a particular sort of magic we get to share that only gets bigger and better the more we share. And who doesn't want life to be a bit more magical?

It is not magic it's God

Life Sucks, Get Supernatural Help

The God of my understanding wants you to know he knows that life is hard. People leave us. Jobs need to change. Sick people hurt us (sometimes physically, sometimes emotionally). There will be people we disagree with and situations we cannot bear to watch. These things happen, and we don't like that they happen, especially to us or those we love. We experience these things in life, but when you write them down, put them in your God Box, and let God take over, somehow, the pain subsides.

The answer and courage to leave a toxic relationship will be given to you when you use a God Box. The animosity you felt towards someone with whom you disagreed starts to diminish. Your feelings of anger, pain, or embarrassment will dissolve away. It helps to remember that people who hurt us might be sick themselves and unaware of what they are doing, but that doesn't mean we need to hang out with or befriend them. Their sickness does not excuse abhorrent behavior. But it does create space in which God can work when you trust in a God Box.

I was a sick, mentally ill man. I was ugly to society. I treated people badly, in stupid and mean ways. I didn't like how most people acted or treated me, so I lashed out. I lived in fear of both failure and success. I was afraid to be alone. When someone did love me, I was irritable and discontented with their company.

Today, I don't throw double cheeseburgers with green chile at McDonald's workers. Today, I didn't go to Walgreens and steal diabetic sticks my drug dealer can sell on eBay. Today, instead, I hold doors open for women. Now, I treat the women in my life with the love and respect they deserve. I am sorry to anyone I have hurt in the past, be it mentally, physically, or emotionally. I ask that you forgive me. From this day on, I pledge to make living amends wherever possible.

I share my past with you because I want you to know how far down the scale in life I went. I had no comprehension of right from wrong. God brought me back to life and restored me to sanity. Imagine what the God of your understanding can do for you.

Unhealthy behaviors can be healed by the simple act of giving them over to God and the God Box. Will everyone be healed that you put in a God Box? Will everyone you add get a new, red Mustang convertible or have their mental health restored? I do not know. God does.

I like to say (and I hope you adopt it into your everyday life too), "I no longer look at what needs to be changed in the world to make me happy. I look at what God needs to change in me to make the world I live in a happier place."

I am now living the life I have always dreamed about. God led others to share the God Box with me. Now I am sharing it with you, so you can share it with others. I hope, together we create a massive ripple effect. Let us pass it on and watch others gain all those things we need or want that could only come from God.

When God shows you love, prosperity, mental and emotional freedom, or even that new Mustang, when God does for you what no one else can, it can only be described in one simple word.

Supernatural.

Don't let that word scare you. When I used to hear it, my first thoughts would be of ghosts and goblins. I thought evil was waiting for me, under my bed or in my closet. Even now, I'm still afraid of the dark and scary movies, but I love to hear a good ghost story to get my heart beating fast. I love to read Stephen King or Dean Koontz to make me shiver with fear.

When I use the word "supernatural," it has a different meaning. It represents a power that is above and beyond the natural world. It is seeing and experiencing phenomena that cannot be explained by ordinary means. It is the hand of God appearing and acting on our behalf. God can heal instantly, change our thoughts, and bring people or circumstances into our lives at the right moment to alter the course of our lives. God can use His supernatural powers when our human efforts fail.

There's a woman named Michele whose story illustrates the process of using the God Box, trusting in Him, and experiencing His supernatural healing power. Michele has been using the God Box for twenty-three years and no longer remembers who first told her about it. She believes in turning her life over to the care of God as she understands Him and finds that writing down her issue and placing it in her God Box is a tangible way for her to let go and let God. She has grown to love God so much that she gets up every morning and communes with God hours before the rest of the world awakens. She says that she was no angel in the past and that drugs and alcohol ruled her life. Today,

Michele is clean and sober and dedicates her life to helping others and giving God all glory. Her friends will tell you that her motto is, "I am beyond grateful to God for everything He has done for me."

Years ago, Michele was in a very abusive marriage. Her husband snorted eight balls of cocaine and chased them with vodka. The cocktail of drugs and alcohol created severe and destructive anger issues. He took out his frustrations on Michele and their children. Their son Todd (not his real name) took the brunt of his beatings in the name of "discipline." Michele and their daughter were also physically and emotionally abused. This man has since passed and will remain anonymous; my intent is not to belittle a once-sick and now-dead man.

As their son, Todd, grew up, he started acting like his father. Todd tore apart doors, punched holes in the walls, and was frighteningly destructive. Whenever there was trouble, Todd was usually in the middle of it. There came a day when Todd was arrested. For what, Michele can no longer remember, since he'd been arrested so many times before. The pain was too great, and she blocked the specifics of this incident from her memory. She does recall that it had to do with drugs or alcohol.

Michele and her daughter picked up Todd from the county jail. Instead of thanking them for their effort, Todd screamed at them. He called them "whore" and other unspeakable names that no mother or sister should ever be called by any man, let alone a son or brother. The experience was atrocious, and Michele saw how out of control Todd was.

Violence, drugs, and alcohol were now Todd's masters. Michele tried to get him help. She took him to a therapist, and though they saw some progress, there were no life-changing revelations. The addiction and anger were still there. He acted the same way his father did. Michele sought out twelve-step programs to help her son. But again, Todd was mired by his own self-destruction.

Todd was headed down a road that inevitably would lead to prison, insanity, or death. As a mother, Michele was desperate for the kind of help that no doctor, relative, or priest could provide. Her son needed a supernatural cleansing of the mind, body, and spirit, and who better to do that than God. Michele wrote her son's name on a piece of paper, folded it, put it in her God Box, and let go. I wish I could tell you she stopped worrying altogether, but she couldn't at first. However, Michele says that she immediately could deal with his behavior more clearly and calmly.

Her stress levels decreased, and her worry over his state of mind and behaviors lessened. She knew her son was sick and needed God's supernatural help. She gave up her most prized possession, her only son, to God's care. In her faith, she found a supply of ease and comfort.

As Michele hoped, Todd started to change. Some behaviors stopped quickly, others more slowly. In God's time and in God's way, Todd transformed.

Today, Todd is a model citizen. God has removed his anger and converted his outlaw spirit. He now gives love where he used to cause pain.

He is a good, honorable son and brother, and a kind, loving husband and father. It would be easy for Michele to take credit for her son's healing, but she doesn't. She gives glory to God and is grateful for her God Box.

Is using a God Box the only answer to life's problems? No—God is the answer. The God Box strengthens my commitment to allow God to take control of my mental wellness, my attitude towards life, and the guy who flipped me the bird for not using my turn signal. I need help with that and much more. God can use His supernatural powers in every aspect of my life, including mental, emotional, and physical wants and needs.

In what aspect of your life do you need supernatural intervention? Do you need spiritual cleansing? Physical healing? Financial stability? Do you have loved ones who are suffering from mental disturbances or addictions? If so, first do the legwork. Consult with a professional if you or someone you know is suffering from a life-threatening illness or is experiencing mental illness. Get help!

God puts good doctors, psychologists, and therapists in our lives so they can help heal us. God does not always heal supernaturally—sometimes, He gives us the tools we need to bring about natural healing. God may choose to perform a miraculous transformation on your loved one, or He may allow that person to continue along their path until they are truly ready to let go of their addiction, anger, or whatever is holding them back.

Some of you may be saying to yourself, "I don't care about this spiritual stuff; I want to be rich." Don't worry—that and more are coming. This part of the book is for those of us who have loved ones needing help from a God with unlimited supernatural power. Many of us have a friend or family member requiring some divine intervention. This part of the book is for you, to give you hope when there seems to be none.

You may ask, "Is it okay to worry about my kids?" I think it's a normal response for most parents to worry about their kids, but it's best to temper your fears as well as you can. Suppose you worry yourself sick to the point of becoming physically or emotionally ill. In that case, you cannot help your loved ones. You need to be mentally sharp to make the right decisions at the right time for whomever you are concerned. If you are distraught and depressed over someone's situation, you will be less effective. Use your God Box to turn your children over to God, then you can stay balanced and healthy enough to make good decisions with a clear, sharp mind.

Do you know what kind of peace comes from freeing yourself from life's worries? Have you experienced the joy and serenity of knowing that the God of wisdom is steering your life in the right direction? It is priceless. It is the beauty of God Box. When you allow God to be the manager of your life, you open the door to His limitless opportunities to act on your behalf, relieve life's burdens, lift your head and heart, and give you hope.

If God can save someone like Todd, imagine what He can do for you and others! God took someone like me—a menace to society who stepped on the toes of others without regard for their welfare or peace of mind—and restored me to an honorable community member. In that case, He is truly the God of the impossible. I used to behave like an animal, but today, I am friends with those I used to think were my enemies: police, judges, and countless others. I was at the bottom of the barrel of life, and God has lifted me to the top. He will do the same for you and your loved ones if you ask Him and allow Him to do His work.

Put that loved one in your God Box, give them to the care of the God of your understanding, then wait and see what happens. I hope all will experience spontaneous healing, but truthfully, I don't believe that will happen. Some of you will. Some will experience healing of the educational variety. For example, God might speak through others. Maybe someone will tell you about a rehab or treatment program now available for someone addicted to drugs or alcohol. Maybe a neighbor will mention that they know the best professional in town to help with a scary diagnosis. God might give you an intuitive thought on your next course of action. God might suddenly make you aware that you are enabling someone's unhealthy behavior, even though you thought you were being helpful. I do not know how God's supernatural ability will manifest in your life—that's between you and your Higher Power.

This might seem out of place, but humor me. Artificial intelligence (AI) is all the rage right now. People say it will be the end of authors like me. Everywhere you look, AI is on the internet. You ask it a question, and suddenly, the answer appears before your eyes. You know what it can't do?

It cannot create a miracle. AI cannot tell a true story like this one. How can AI know what it's truly like to feel lonely? How can AI know what real desperation is? No artificial intelligence can heal our loved ones or tell us what it is like to be human. I trust God with my life, not AI. God's way has always worked better than anything I or anyone else could have planned. If God can move mountains and make heaven and earth, He can restore us to a life worth living. AI will never be able to do that.

God wants us to be happy, loving, and free from worry. Why wallow in pain and needless suffering when God waits for you to call on Him? I thank God in advance for those He is about to heal with His supernatural power and love, because I know he will do so. God's supernatural power can heal you and your loved ones. Learn to walk hand in hand with the God of your understanding. Trust Him and see His amazing love and power. It's not mere luck or coincidence that heals or brings good fortune. It is Him, in his supernatural power and being, that can improve your life.

Pen to paper time.

Write down the name of the person that you worry over most in your life, whether it's because they have issues as severe as I once did, they just lost their job, or maybe it's even something smaller. It doesn't matter why you worry over them, just write their name down and give it to your God Box. Next, and here's the hard part, I want you to wait and see. Something will come along to ease your worry and their burden. That's the power of God and your God Box.

Add anyone, anything, to your God Box

God's Voodoo

Truthfully, I like to call God's supernatural work "God's Voodoo." I do not know how God works or why He does what He does. When I ask for His help, God moves heaven and earth to bring me what I need, and I call that God's Voodoo. The general definition of voodoo is a religious practice combining Roman Catholic ritual elements with African magical and religious rites. But that's not what I mean here. And I get it—using this word might offend some folks, and that's not what I aim to do. The last thing I'd ever want to do is hurt somebody's feelings or have them think I'm making fun of them or their cultural practices. Generally, I try to only make fun of myself, I promise. Let me explain.

I do not want to call what God does for us "magic" though I've done so in previous chapters. That's why I waited for these pages to explain myself. Magic is a trick. Magic is a form of entertainment using misdirection. The magician gets you to look over there while the real trick is happening right before your eyes. What God is doing for you and me is no trick. So, then what is it? Now that my mind is clear and I have an unbelievable relationship with God, I know what it is. It is, without question, a blessing from God.

The thing God does with the God Box is a blessing. He gives us His favor and protection in many ways. God gives us His support, approval, guidance, and help in whatever endeavor we seek in his intercession. Big or small, His blessings happen every day.

Why does God do that Voodoo he does so well for us? Because He loves us and wants what is best for us. Because when we ask for His blessings, He wants to give them to us.

My body, mind, and soul are ignited when I write my request on paper and put it in my God Box. God tells me it demonstrates my commitment to Him and to the process.

God wants people to love Him and follow Him. He wants us to show others the same kind of love, mercy, and forgiveness He has shown us. God wants us to know He loves and cares for His children. God wants us to have conversations with Him, to not only talk to Him, but listen to Him as well. God wants us to have meaningful work, relationships, and adventures.

God has inspired me to write this book and wants me to share it with everyone, regardless of their religious or spiritual principles. The God of my understanding wants you to grow closer to the God of your understanding. God wants to free your mind from worry, pain, and despair. I want you to have what has been so freely given to me. God has worked His special Voodoo on me, and I am so full of love, joy, and happiness that I feel I'll burst if I don't share it with you!

I have to let you know that my relationship with God has not always been so peachy keen. There have been days when God was not pleased with my behavior, and trust me, He let me know. By various means, God showed me that He was unhappy with how I treated others and myself. No one has hurt, mistreated, belittled, or abused me as severely as I have done to myself. Time and again, my self-negative thoughts nearly killed me.

Yes, I even tried ending my life on more than the one occasion previously mentioned.

I am happy to report with the help of therapy and God's grace, I no longer harm myself or others. Do I ever get down? Yes. Life happens and things upset me. I have moments of anxiety and depression, but those kinds of thoughts used to happen constantly. Now, in those moments, I write down what's swirling in my mind and put those slips of paper into my Box. And boom! God does for me what I can't do for myself by refocusing me or scrubbing those thoughts away. Those bouts of depression, anxiety, and thoughts of unworthiness go into my God Box, and God restores me.

God sent the right therapist into my life at the right time to help me get on the proper medication to ease the pain I was causing in my mind. Is that God's Voodoo? You better believe it. God gave me the courage to get help and to seek professional intervention. Without question, God has restored my sanity.

There was a moment when I was lost. Okay, it was more than a moment— more like four years. I lost my sense of reality. I hated God passionately and blamed Him for my divorce, drug addiction, and mental illness. I blamed Him for the problems I caused in my life. I was wanted by the police for cashing forged checks and using fake identification, and somehow that was God's fault. My wife at the time filed for divorce, and with good reason. I was a drunk, a drug addict, stealing money from casinos and other places. Was this my fault? Yes, it was. Yet I refused to take personal responsibility for my actions and the situations I encountered. I blamed it all on God, as so many of us do.

One day, while wasted on bargain-basement gin and my never-ending fury, I went over to my brother Chris's apartment. He had an old beat-up couch with cigarette burns on the cushions, and honestly not much else. Oh, there was more furniture and things. But I remember the couch. And I remember my brother. Chris was the kindest, gentlest man alive. He never hurt a fly. That man had a love, warmth, and compassion within him for which we should all strive. He did not have a lot of material possessions, but what he had, he shared with anyone who was in need.

And he loved to give a hug. A hug from Chris was as close to experiencing unconditional love as possible. God rest his sweet soul.

I sat in Chris's room, snorting cocaine cut with baby powder. Drug dealers who cut their drugs suck. I drank seven miniatures of V.O. whisky for good measure. I was high as Ben Franklin's kite and drunk as a skunk that fell into a barrel of booze. I went on a rant, a vicious verbal attack on God like you never heard. I called Him foul words and names. Words inappropriate to have in a book about God and a Box. I yelled and swung in the air at a God who failed me. My thoughts weren't necessarily coherent, but they sure were focused on blame. *He let me down! How could a God who loves, a God of second chances, be so vengeful? He let my wife divorce me, and a warrant's out for my arrest. I'm addicted to meth, cocaine, and alcohol! How can He let me act like a savage animal?*

I screamed, "I hate You, God!" Then a miracle happened. God spoke through my brother and showed me what I could not see.

The door to my brother's room opened, and Chris stuck his head out and said, "At least you're still talking to Him." Such gentle words, and they still hold me to this day. Then Chris smiled his innocent smile and closed the door. *Wow,* I thought to myself, *Chris is right.* I was still talking to God. *I must believe in Him if I'm talking to Him.* I sat on the bed and cried, begging forgiveness for being such a fool.

Today I know God is real.

The God you believe in and the God I believe in is real. He shows Himself to us in so many ways—as he did for me in Chris's hugs, words, and smile. God is wise and omnipotent beyond anything we can imagine. His power and strength are limitless. His desire to heal and supply guidance is infinite.

If you read anything in this book that you find enlightening, earth-shattering, insightful, or spiritual, the glory goes to God. God is the one who is writing this book; I am merely the vessel He is using to share His message. God wants you to know that this book is for everyone, regardless of religious or spiritual beliefs. God wants you to know He loves you, and even if you do not believe in Him, He believes in you.

I used the phrase God's Voodoo when I started this journey because I didn't know what else to call it. It's that thing God does when you ask for His help, and He obliges with wisdom and strength. I have shared my story with a room full of twenty to thirty friends and told them how God saved a man like me: homeless, addicted to drugs, and completely broken spiritually, mentally, and emotionally. God did for me what I was unable to do for myself. God restored my life, sanity, and health in two years and gave me more than I could have ever imagined. I married a fantastic woman October 2023, and now we have a house and a car that are both paid for. I have an excellent relationship with my daughter—who, in 2020, told me she never wanted to speak to me again. God has healed my mind, and I have been writing screenplays, a children's story, and this book, God's gift to those who suffer or need guidance and wisdom.

The changes in my life accelerated when I started to use a God Box to give my life over to the care of God. In God's hands, I receive hope, love, guidance, a new way of thinking, and a new way of being. I am continually receiving God's blessings. Though I might revert to calling it what I once did every now and then, I see what his work should be called now: not God's Voodoo, but God's Blessings. Accept them and Him as I have, and you'll see it. You'll feel it. You'll know it with the same confidence I do.

What do we do next? If you're like me, maybe you're a little peckish. Let's find some nourishment, or maybe something just good and sweet. I've always been partial to doughnuts.

Bring the Doughnuts

My good friend, Scooter, and I were sitting in a meeting of a group of friends. I wanted a sweet treat; most days, when these friends gathered, some old soul brought doughnuts. I waited and waited for someone to show up with some. I explained to Scooter I was mad that no one brought any of the delectable treats—iced, glazed, filled, rolled in nuts—I wasn't picky! I just wanted a doughnut!

Let me fill you in on Scooter. He's one of my life advisors and I'm always thankful for him. Scooter's an eighty-four-year-old Native American whose wisdom exceeds any pastor, reverend, or spiritual leader I have ever known. "Scooter" is a nickname he got from riding around on his motor scooter every day, everywhere. His real name is Rick (but mum's the word—don't tell anyone).

Scooter said, "If you want doughnuts, why don't you bring the doughnuts?" Seems obvious, right? But it blew my mind. Not only did he mean it in a literal sense, but as a metaphor for how to engage in the world. If I want love in the world, why don't I bring love? If I want compassion in this crazy world, why don't I give compassion? As simple as it sounded, I had never looked at it that way. Bring to the world what I want out of the world… If I want doughnuts, why don't I bring the doughnuts?

What a simple and priceless spiritual principle! Wouldn't it be great if everyone practiced this every day? You might think you're already doing that, and no doubt some of you are in varying degrees. We must practice what we preach, give what we want to receive, and always ask for what is best in situations that cause pain, frustration, and discomfort.

No more of that "Do as I say, not what I do" kind of attitude. God wants us to help others do amazing things and help the elderly with our time and resources. God wants us to bring the love we want, the stuff we crave or need. If you ask your God Box for more money, hedge your bet by giving some of the money you now have. It doesn't have to be oodles—just a bit will do. Show God you are a good steward with what you have and watch how your life fill with nifty goods and trinkets.

What kind of help am I giving to others suffering mentally, emotionally, or physically? I need to be to others what I want others to be for me and my loved ones. Most of us know the Golden Rule, but if you need a reminder, it's "Do unto others as you would have them do unto you." It's golden for a reason.

What favor, grace, or blessing are you asking God for in your Box? How do you want the world to treat you? How do you want others to behave? Do you want peace, love, and harmony? I know I do. Are you bringing peace, love, and harmony to others? Are you bringing the doughnuts?

When someone tries to cut you off in traffic, do you give them room to merge, or do you get angry, honk your horn, roll down the window, and cuss them out? Do you speed up to block their way in? Are you entitled to that spot? I know in the past, if you cut me off in traffic, it was on. I was going to chase you down, belittle you, and tell you how I felt about it. I would show you street-justice for disrespecting me. I'm glad those days are behind me.

Do I ever get frustrated with the problems of the world: wars, hate crimes, political divisions? I sure do. Can I change the world? Can you? Maybe. Maybe not. The only thing I can change is my attitude and outlook on life. As I change myself, I subtly have an impact on those around me. It creates a ripple effect. I change the world around me by being a good example. If I want love in the world, I must show love in the ways that God and my God Box have taught me. God has brought good men and women into my life to teach me how to behave like a child of God. God and my God Box have brought love into my life in ways I never thought possible.

Before my wife and I were blessed with a car, I took public transportation. While waiting for the bus, a young man in his early twenties, and obviously high on drugs, accidentally bumped into me. To me, he was clearly on methamphetamine. He was tweaking, his body spasms uncontrollable. After he bumped into me, he apologized, and I smiled to acknowledge I understood it was an accident. As I turned away, he suddenly clocked me with a right to the jaw. I stumbled back, shocked at his attack.

I was a violent man at one time, and this was a violent encounter. My first reaction was to strike back and unload with a vengeance. Fortunately for those involved, God spoke to me through a friend the day before and gave me a new way of looking at life. I heard these words, which became one of my life's mission statements, "Others first."

My friend Anthony told me when situations were not going my way, to think, "Others first," and then act like I meant it. Was I supposed to use this now, after getting punched in my face? How can I say, "Others first" when the other in question just assaulted me? I was on a mission from God. To write this book and change myself and the world around me. If I wanted love and forgiveness from others, I needed to show that same love and forgiveness, even as I rubbed my jaw.

For the first time, I can honestly say I put others first. I looked at that man and acknowledged to myself he was mentally ill. I let it go. I didn't strike back. I didn't retaliate as I would have in the past. I let that man go on his way.

I called my wife, crying, and told her how I was assaulted at the bus stop while I stood there minding my own business. Today I know those tears were not because of the physical pain in my mouth. I was crying because I felt compassion for the first time when I saw my fellow man the way God wanted me to see him. I want to have love and peace in my world, and I brought the doughnuts that day.

I must be what I want out of the world and others. I must be what I ask God and my God Box for. It is the law of attraction; peace comes to those who offer peace, and love comes to those who show love. My wife says energy, good or bad, takes the path of least resistance. Love, kindness, and generosity towards each other create a path of least resistance. Anger and hate use up energy. Anger is a learned behavior that I no longer choose to engage in these days. Life is about bringing doughnuts. It is about being an example to others of how we can ideally treat one another.

You can share what you have with others. You can share what you learn with others. You can share a smile or a kind word, a sandwich or change for the bus. Big or small, the possibilities are endless. There is unlimited potential at your disposal that you can use to help yourself or others. Sharing only gets easier with a God Box. You can ask for even more to share. Or you can ask for selfish things like I did. Sometimes I can't help but hope somebody shows up with a raspberry-filled jelly roll or a Boston cream.

This next story is not about doughnuts. It is a story about cake. More precisely, it's about how I was selfish and self-centered when it came to cake. Maybe I have a problem with sweets. But that's not the point either. Or maybe it is. Maybe now I'm thinking about delicious cake… Wait! Get back on track, Mark.

One day I was sitting in a group of alcoholics and addicts learning to stay clean and sober. I was new in recovery and had a self-centered attitude towards life. Life was about me and what it had to offer me. "I better get mine before you get yours" was the mission statement of the day, long before, "Others first."

The group of men and women I shared the room was celebrating sober anniversaries. We commemorate these special days by giving them medallions (a coin or "chip") with the number of months or years they have been sober inscribed. We also celebrate by serving cake. It is a significant accomplishment for an alcoholic or addict to completely abstain from alcohol or drugs for a whole month, a series of months, a year, or more. We party down! Of course, our parties can't really involve popping the bubbly—that would be counterproductive. So, we feast on cake.

The volunteer who brought the cake picked a special ice cream cake from Baskin Robbins. My favorite! There were thirteen lucky people present and eighteen pieces of cake. I was first to finish my piece, and oh my goodness, it was delicious. The cake and ice cream mixture in my mouth tasted like heaven, and I wanted more. The meeting chairman announced we could go back for seconds after we waited for the latecomers to get a piece of cake. I wanted to rush to the table and grab another piece of that terrific ice cream cake before it was gone, but I had to wait. The people who were late started to file in slowly. First one, then another, then a third. The ice cream cake was going fast; only a few lovely big pieces were left. I wanted one, but those darn people kept coming in and grabbing plates.

I couldn't control the situation, but I had access to a power that could—God. I could pray that no one else would come in, and I did that. I asked God to keep anyone else away from the meeting so I could have another piece of cake. I wanted God to prevent someone else from coming into the meeting to seek recovery or to celebrate an unbelievable accomplishment, so I could stuff my own face. I prayed for it, and I meant it.

How selfish and self-centered can one guy get, huh? Back then, I viewed my God as a God of good possessions and tasty treats. Others had their own God; they could get their own ice cream cake. After waiting another twenty minutes, God gave me that extra piece of cake. I ate it and enjoyed it. At that time, it was more important to me to get extra ice cream cake than to see someone recover from a hopeless state of addiction. I hate to admit it, but I didn't care; I wanted what I wanted without regard for anyone else's wants and needs.

God and I have since talked about this. I was wrong, and I'm sorry for asking what I did. With God and my God Box, my life has changed regarding my selfish and self-centered behaviors. God used my wife to teach me that when I pray, my requests are answered only if they are for the highest good for all. Let that sink in, and keep in mind—I got my piece of cake.

My request to the God of my understanding should only be granted if it is for the good of all. Not for me, or for you, *for all*. I can't wrap my head around deciding what is best for everyone, so I let God decide. God knows what is best for me, you, and everyone with whom I interact daily. I trust God to make those decisions that used to confuse me. And I think God granted me that slice of cake so I learned this valuable lesson.

Let's look at an example: suppose I use my God Box to ask God for more money without adding the intention that it be "for the highest good for all." I could be in a world of hurt. I might get more money, but it might come from a death in the family. A parent might meet an untimely death and leave me an inheritance. I do not want that kind of blessing. Yes, I want more money, but not at the expense of someone else's life.

With the intention for the highest good for all, the extra money might come from any number of places. You could hit the lottery. God might motivate your employer to give you a raise. You may find a Picasso at a garage sale that you buy for five dollars and sell for $50,000. If your request is not selfish like mine was, you will enjoy it more than ice cream cake. I can assure you. God will know if you ask for thoughtless gifts or for opportunities and gifts that will help others as well as you. We want to receive blessings and favor but not at someone else's expense.

Think about your intentions as you put pen to paper. Yes, you can be selfish sometimes, but not all the time. If you do, eventually you'll get to eat all the cake by yourself because you won't have anyone with which to share it. And if you didn't know, that's why they make cakes big. They're meant to be shared, as are all His Blessings.

I am happy to report that I now have my cake and get to eat it too. Cheeky, I know. Who would ever have guessed that cake and doughnuts could help change lives? Of course, we might be called upon to do a little more than simply dig into the sweet stuff.

Work

Mary, one of my mom's friends, was married blissfully for thirty years. Then her husband unexpectedly died. After a few years of mourning her beloved Tom, Mary told my mom she prayed for another husband. She was lonesome and missed the companionship of married life. She prayed for love for two years, not for some fancy house on the beach or some other outlandish request. Mary only wanted someone that could spend the rest of their years together, cozily and happily, a man to love and cherish. She loved being married and wanted again to be someone's wife, but no potential husband surfaced. She could not understand why God wasn't answering her prayers. Now, Mary was one of the most spiritual women I've ever met. She read her good book and prayed on her knees daily. She did everything she could think of to win God's favor. God refused to bless her with her heart's one desire.

One day my mom visited Mary at her modest house. Mary cried to my mom that she wanted to be married again. Mom listened as Mary explained she was at a loss, at her wit's end. She didn't know why God was testing her.

With remarkable tact, my mom finally said, "Mary, the only way you'll get your prayers answered is if the mailman proposes." You see, Mary hardly left the house. She was afraid to meet new people so making new friends was out of the question. If a man bade hello to her at a store or Bible study, her response was minimum. How was God supposed to grant her the thing she wanted so badly if she was not going to participate? Even a little? Just a smidge? Mom suggested she join a social group, try online dating, and put herself out there in the stream of life so she could meet people. But Mary didn't want to do the work.

I think you're sharp enough to get the point: God might want you to work to get your prayers answered. He will not make you chase it. That is one thing I can tell you for sure—God will never make you chase or beg for His help. Work for it? Yes. Chase after it? No. God does not want you to beg for wisdom, support, or courage. Ask God for it, trust Him, and let it go. Rinse and repeat, if necessary, but never beg.

Only evil spirits respond to begging, and I suggest you avoid going down that rabbit hole. Ask God and be willing to do the footwork if He wants that of you. Keep in mind that sometimes God's answer is simply, "No." Assume it is a solid no. I'm sure it will save you from some unforeseen pain.

Am I telling you that you must work to receive God's blessings? Not necessarily. However, you might have to start a YouTube channel or change careers to make that dream come true. Put your request in the God Box and check in with God to motivate you to act.

For me, blessings and favors rolled in. Some I asked for, others I did not. God gave me peace of mind, serenity, and goodwill toward others; I didn't even know I needed them. I thought I was the poster child for sound mental health. God handed me favor He stored away for me and was waiting for me to be willing to receive it! God sent me material things, but the most significant blessings were and are intangible:

- A stress-free life
- Love and tolerance of others
- Comfort in knowing I am safe in God's arms

I now look at the world differently. I have compassion and love for others that I never thought was possible. Does God help with emotional well-being? Absolutely!

Every day my health, money, friends, and family improve and grow in ways only a God with supernatural powers can achieve. God will open doors for you—it's your job to walk through them.

I now trust God with my entire life, not only the people and situations that bother me. I trusted Him with my housing needs, and now I have a permanent roof over my head. I asked God to bring me joy and happiness, and I am overflowing with both! I used my God Box to petition God to teach me to see the world through His eyes instead of my pain-filled, hateful eyes. He guides me every day. But I must do the work. I can't stand on the sidelines in my own life and expect the score to change.

When I prayed that God restore my mental health, He assembled a fantastic team of professionals to help me heal. But God doesn't wake me up for appointments; I set the alarm, get out of bed, dress, and leave the house to get help from that team. When I had no car, it was up to me to ride the bus to Health Care for the Homeless each week to meet with them. There were days I had to drag myself out of bed and lug myself to the bus stop, but God gave me the strength to carry on when I was ready to quit. God gave me the courage to forge on, face my demons, and overcome them. I needed to try do something with that courage, even if it was simply showing up.

God told me He wants me to write this book. But this book is not writing itself. I work eight hours a day, six days a week to get words on the page. Nevertheless, God has brought together a fantastic group of people who work behind the scenes reading, editing, and helping me with this project. God has given me a team of family and friends who encourage and support this cause. I am the one who tunes in to God and types out the ideas He wants me to share with you. I do the work, and I do it with such joy and happiness that it hardly seems like work most days.

Are you willing to do the work? Are you willing to change, grow, and allow God to stretch you? If you're not ready, that's okay. A bigger house, faster car, or someone to love is still on the way. However, if you are like me and want an incredible, extravagant lifestyle, with trips to Paris while flying first class (not coach—I need some legroom), a million dollars, and a penthouse full of cut-crystal chandeliers and a closet full of tailored suits (with Italian leather shoes tucked on shelves below), be ready to do a little work. Why settle for good when you can have great? Better yet, why settle for great when you can have only the best? God tells me daily that He has so much more for me if I am willing to do the work. I could sit back and enjoy the good fortune God has brought me, or I could sit back and enjoy the greater fruits of the labor of God.

Do I want more of what God has in store for me? You bet I do! Am I delighted with where I am at this time in my life? You better believe I am! God says He has a bigger and better life for me, not only cars, houses, and cash (some gold would be lovely too—nuggets or bars, I'm not picky), but even more. He wants me to have a stronger foundation based on my spiritual beliefs. Because of the Blessings he's already showered on me, I can now see life through a different lens than I ever could before. My old vision was warped, twisted from anger and pain. But now everything is clear, and I see the beauty in all God's creations, from the towering mountains to the desert pocket mouse. Looking through this lens not only helps me see beauty, but helps me understand the world more clearly as well. God wants me to take part in the process. He wants me to try. Sometimes—not always—he wants me to do a little work.

I want everyone to experience what I have. I wake up every morning looking forward to what God, my God Box, and the day have in store for me. Material goods and money appear because of what I have requested in my God Box. I turn my needs over to God, and checks arrive in the mail. People have given me brand-new shoes just when I needed a pair, sometimes without even using my God Box. Opportunities arose I never imagined would. People show up in my life and help set the stage for the next phase of my development, including writing this book. I cannot explain it. But I've said it before and I'm sure to say it again, I don't understand all of the majesty of God. He's impossible to fully comprehend, at least for someone like me. And I have no idea what your God has in store for you, but I know whatever it is, it's going to be amazing.

Do you have to be open to what the God Box can do for you? Open enough to be willing to give it a try. Will you get rich and famous by using a God Box? God's favors might require a little work on your part. As the saying goes: "You can't win the lottery if you don't buy a ticket." Purchasing a ticket is the work. Do you want to be a movie star? God may require you to attend casting calls or take an acting class. Do you want to be a rock icon? Better practice your guitar and be ready to take some gigs at crummy bars for a while. Maybe you don't need your face on magazine covers, but you're looking for something different—an exciting new career in an unfamiliar field. God might want you to become an apprentice in a shop or go to school to learn a new trade. And while you're at school, you might meet your future employer or best friend or spouse—God might line up answers to a dozen prayers while you think you're doing the work to get one prayer answered.

Will God make you wait for the favors you request in your God Box? Only God knows His timing. Your blessing could be seconds, days, or weeks away. Do not give up five minutes before the miracle happens. Know that God has your best interest at heart. Let the God of your understanding be the one to guide you through an intuitive thought or the sound advice of another. Is it a sign you have been looking for?

Here it is:

GOD IS REAL.

Keep pursuing your dreams. Place your wants and needs in your God Box and wait to see what happens. Do the work that God asks of you. Enjoy the peace that comes with trusting that God is in control. Being happy to do the work makes the work easier, but that all comes from attitude. And if you've been paying attention, you know I was once in need of a big attitude adjustment.

Your God Box can be unique to you

Thoughts and Perceptions

"Life sucks," is something I used to say all the time. Some of you are thinking or saying something similar daily. In the past, I told myself I was not worthy of a relationship with God, friends, or family. I was simply existing, barely surviving—I did not engage in or enjoy my life. And, as I said, life sucked.

It sure did, but it was my fault that it sucked so bad.

I told my daughter I hated her. I did drugs and drank alcohol to excess. I did not go to my spiritual house to commune with God. I acted like a fool and was on a self-destructive mission. My thoughts and feelings were negative, and I did not think life offered love and compassion. I thought life was cruel and that God hated me. I thought God didn't want to have anything to do with me. I didn't think I wanted anything to do with Him.

I did not know God's gifts and favor were there the whole time. I was too sick to see what God could do for me and felt unworthy to ask for good things. Instead, I prayed every night to die in my sleep, for something, someone—Him or otherwise—to put me out of my misery.

Today, I wake up and cannot wait to see what new adventure God has in store for me. I can hardly wait to get to my computer to write and work on a screenplay, a children's book, or this very manuscript. But I do wait because first, I have to chit-chat with God. I do not use the word "talk" with my God because that is not what we do—we chit-chat. It's like being with my best friend, sharing thoughts and ideas. We do not call each other "thee" and "thou." My God straight-up tells me like it is. He tells me, "Mark, stop doing that," or he whispers, "Mark, start making this," and sometimes he even says, "Mark, I'm proud of you." Nothing fancy. Just God and one of His many children chit-chatting about what's going on in life. I highly recommend you spend time with your Higher Power each morning. Even if He doesn't seem to answer back, I assure you, He's listening.

When I start my morning seeking God's wisdom and guidance, it sets the tone for the rest of my day. I ask and He tells; He tells and I listen. That way, my thoughts and feelings are raised to a higher plane, and I can set out on the right foot. Life starts not to suck so bad.

After my conversation with God, I watch the morning news with Gale King. The news is not always rosy, but I put the world's troubles in my God Box and ask God to guide my thoughts, and there I am, once again, looking at life differently. When I allow God to shape my thoughts, my perceptions become more spiritual, and I proceed to act from a more spiritual basis.

You can devise a million reasons why God will never give you what you want and need. I am telling you to lose that attitude right now!

Those negative thoughts and perceptions need to go by the wayside immediately. Use your God Box to be rid of them. Your mind needs to be sharp, clear, and enthusiastic about life and what God has in store for you. Whether rich or poor, it doesn't matter how good or bad you have been. You are a child of God—now act like it!

My mom used to tell me that I was the son of the King of Kings, so I should act like it. She tried to teach me to walk into a room of people with my head up and my shoulders back and greet everyone as if they too were royalty. I want everyone to feel the love and joy within me these days when I walk into a room.

I am not cocky or stuck up about it. Trust me—I'm no Brad Pitt. But, you know what? Brad Pitt is no Mark Martinez, either!

I am one of God's children, and you are too. Even if you aren't feeling it, start acting like it—your negative thoughts and perceptions will begin to change. I love people, and people love me (not everyone, of course, and that's okay). If I'm doing the next right thing for the highest good for all, and I don't interfere with another's peace of mind, then I'm not concerned with what others think of me. Focus on learning God's will for you, keep your thoughts and perceptions positive, and do God's bidding. God will show you more and more favor, grace, and, finally, love.

Regarding love, many good women who loved me have come and gone in my life. I pushed them away for multiple reasons. I thought I would never find a woman to love me who would be faithful and true again. I thought God didn't want me to have love, and who was I to deserve love when I couldn't even love myself? I even swore I would never marry again. *Who wants to be tied down like that? Why should I have to answer to anybody? I'm a grown man and can take care of myself! I'm better off alone anyways, since I'd probably get cheated on in the end.* These were my thoughts and beliefs regarding love and marriage.

Here I am today, married to a woman who, I am one hundred percent certain, loves me unconditionally.

God sent Christie into my life when I needed help and love. I was newly clean and sober, and COVID restrictions were in place. I met Christie through a group of friends who were helping me with my sobriety. She walked into the room, and we have been inseparable since. I could share with her the mental and emotional pain I was going through. Without question, I did not deserve another chance at love, yet there she was, staring me in the face. God sent her into my life at precisely the right time. God knows what He's doing.

I know Christie will never cheat on me. In fact, I feel sorry for any man or woman who might try to seduce her. Christie is a tough cookie and would never stand for it. She lifts me up. She has my back. She encourages my writing and everything I do when I am pursuing the highest good for all. She supports me in ways I never could have imagined. I don't feel tied down, I feel like I have a shared and happy home. I asked her to marry me, even though I had sworn I would never marry again. While I was wrong in most of thinking when it came to remarrying, I was right about being a grown man, and grown-ups are allowed to change their minds. I'm so happy that my obstinate nature didn't stand in my way or in the path of God's plan for me.

Without her, this book would never have existed—after all, Christie's the one who introduced me to the God Box. God brought love into my life and motivated me to act for the greater good of all. Now I get to share this life-changing book. Better yet, I get to share my days with Christie, the love of my life.

But my terrible behavior didn't only affect my romantic life. I was destructive in relationships with most of the important women I've known and who dared to love me. I've mentioned before that my daughter cut off contact with me. I acted out in so many ugly ways, I can't fault Monique for that decision. I once told Monique she was no longer my child because she refused to lend me money that she knew I would use for drugs. She told me she never wanted to see me again, and I knew she meant it this time. My thoughts were ugly and hateful towards life and everyone in it, including myself. I knew I deserved to be cut off from her life, but that didn't instantly make me change my ways and become the father she always deserved. I don't know if I'll ever really be the father my beautiful Monique deserves, but I'm miles closer today than I was then.

I'm happy to report that I now have a healthy relationship with Monique, made stronger by God's grace. I didn't do anything to deserve her love again after all the terrible things I'd put her through, but I couldn't help missing her, worrying about her, wishing I could ask her how her day was. I chose to rely on God and placed my daughter's name in my God Box, and God started working to change how I think. My perception of life shifted, my behavior changed, and somehow Monique became aware that I was no longer the person I used to be. I know there are a lot of you who have trouble with your children. Please, believe those relationships can change. Give your child over to the care of the God of your understanding and your God Box and wait for spectacular life to flourish. Surrounded by good family, how could life suck?

I cannot tell you exactly what made Monique change her mind to trust and love me again. Hearing that I'd changed couldn't have been enough. But I know this: God did what I could not do. God knew I would not go on without the love and understanding of my daughter and grandson.

God gave me grace when I did not deserve it. Somehow, he instilled that grace within my daughter so that she took another chance on me. Once, I was an utter embarrassment to her. Now Monique and I visit weekly, talk daily, and she's helping edit this book.

Life doesn't suck anymore. No, not at all—life is grand! Life is full of miracles and beauty and love! I wish I could scream it from every roof and mountaintop, but instead of risking a charge for disturbing the peace, I'm getting the message out to you, right now, on these pages.

God can show you grace and favor no matter how far down in life you have gone and regardless of where you are now. God can give you everything your heart desires and more. He can restore relationships that seem fathoms beyond repair. God's miracles are real. I know, and so will you.

The first thing you can do is shift your attitude. Our outcomes begin with our thoughts and perceptions. If you choose to do so, the change starts here and now.

My friend Karl always made controversial statements (hence his nickname, Controversial Karl). One day he shared how he found a new way to look at life. What he said made a lot of sense. No controversy (for once), only sound advice God shared with me through this man. Controversial Karl said, "Christmas is a state of mind."

I am someone who happens to love Christmas. My ears perked up.
I love going to the store to buy presents for others. I love the smell of a fresh Christmas tree. I love seeing family and friends through the season. I love the scent of Christmas sugar cookies baking in the oven, anticipating the moment they'll be cool enough to eat. Listening to Christmas music lifts my spirits. Just thoughts of candy canes and Santa Claus and watching Christmas movies I've seen thirty times and wondering what cakes or sweet treats might be at a gathering and CK! (figure it out) I love it all. That's a life that doesn't suck.

Some people have a bah-humbug attitude towards Christmas. They hate having to spend time with family or going to parties and festivities. They think Christmas is a gimmick that department stores made up to increase profits.

Crowded malls, grocery stores packed with people, spoiled children (or adults) throwing fits that they didn't get the newest game console—they paint holiday pictures in their heads with the grimmest brushes, dipped in black coal dust instead of gumdrop reds, greens, and yellows.

But me? My head is full of dancing sugar plums and merry elves. I see towering Christmas trees and hear Santa's sleighbells. The holiday pictures in my head are vibrant and musical, filling me with the warm-fuzzies I wish everyone could feel.

It's all about perception. When Controversial Karl said, "Christmas is a state of mind," the only controversy for me was that it took me so long to discover the truth. And the truth is, if you love Christmas, you can experience that kind of joy every single day.

If you hate Christmas, you are also welcome to experience that negativity every day. It depends on your state of mind. December 25th is really only a date on a calendar. For those of you who don't celebrate Christmas, I'm sure you have a holiday that you look forward to as much as I do Christmas. Unfortunately, that means some of you also dread that day as much as the other members of your faith or family gleefully anticipate it. Whatever the day or date is, it's the way we look at it and how we approach it that makes a difference.

On Christmas day, I see my daughter, and we open presents. I revel in her delight as she opens the gifts I give her. If I want to experience more of that kind of happiness, I can visit her and take a small miracle any day of the year. If I want to be miserable and complain about the world's ways, I don't have to wait until Christmas to be a Scrooge. I can experience that misery every day if I choose.

You can have whatever kind of day you want.

Every day can be Christmas. Love it or hate it—it depends on you. God likes to give us good things, so why not accept them cheerfully? How would you feel if you gave someone a new car and they complained about the color? It happens all the time. God gives us a gift and it's not exactly the way we wanted it. It could have been more or different.

Look at it like this: How long would you continue to bake cookies for your co-workers if they never thanked you? What if they also always told you they'd prefer chocolate chip instead of oatmeal? And that this isn't how their grandmothers used to make them? After repeatedly getting that kind of reception, you might say, "Get your own cookies!"

On the other hand, if your co-workers' responses were focused on how much they love these cookies and they thanked you (not up and down, but simply and plainly), you'd probably keep baking and bringing them in. I know if someone likes my cookies, I step up the whole operation; I make Mom's secret-recipe pineapple upside-down cake to share with them. Even if it is a bit of a pain to make, and the ingredients are a little expensive, I'm happy to do it because they appreciated my cookies and the effort I put in to make them.

Well, God feels the same way. Accept God's gifts with gratitude and joy. God's gifts can come swiftly and with brilliance when we have the right attitude. I didn't get clean and sober to be miserable. God did not restore me to sanity so I could have a sucky life. God did not drag me out of the gutter to hear me whine and complain that I wanted chocolate chips instead of oatmeal.

I look forward to what God has in store for me each day. I'm optimistic and focused on today and the gifts it will bring.

I can have Christmas every day, be it February 1st or July 19th.

Appreciate the apartment or house you live in. Be grateful you have a place to live. I may not live in a mansion, but it feels like a mansion to me. I'm thankful it has heating and cooling. I can take a hot shower. I have a refrigerator full of food. My love and I can watch scary movies on a big screen TV, bundled up safe and sound, without fear that someone will jump out and hurt us.

Go to work with a smile. I know a bunch of people who cannot work and would love to be able to earn money and contribute to society. If you don't like your job, find a job you want, or find purpose in the position you already have.

I look forward to going to work each day and see it as a privilege rather than a chore because I didn't work for years. I slept the day through, did drugs, and got drunk. It was a joyless existence. Now I joyfully put in long hours each day, helping others, and working on this book. Is this book going to change the world? I don't know. If I had to make a prediction, I'd guess that it won't. But I do know it can change *your* world.

Life isn't always easy. You and I both know that. Yet, I continue to look forward to the gifts coming with the excitement of a child waiting for Christmas morning. Those gifts might not be a mansion, cars, money, or the newest game console, but instead love, joy, and the new, refreshing moments God has for me. He has them for you too.

You may think you don't deserve good things, but God is a God of forgiveness and love—as well as grace. God has forgiven you for your past, so it's time to forgive yourself. If you cheated on your spouse or stole vitamins from Walmart, make a living amends. You can start today to become a better person.

If you don't love life, make it a goal. Jumpstart that good feeling by helping others.

Start small if you must, by saying hello to a stranger or buying someone a cup of coffee. Stop antagonizing those who you think deserve punishment. Slowly, try to build up to bigger and better things. You could volunteer for your favorite cause—again, you can start in smaller ways, like helping out on a phone bank (you don't even have to get dressed or leave the house for those). Write a thank-you note to someone who has helped you. Call a friend who may be down and tell them you're grateful for their friendship. I like to do that, and it makes me feel good to let my friends know I appreciate them. Whatever ways you can manage to impact the lives of others positively are fine. They're more than that—they're awesome! I never would have thought it just a few years ago, but I've discovered that nothing makes me feel better than helping others.

You deserve happiness, confidence, and joy, even if you believe you do not. Open the channel to receive God's blessings by being grateful. Focus on the positive relationships or hip, slick, fabulous things you have right now and be thankful for whatever else God sends your way. Tell Him, "Thank You," and express to Him your gratitude.

You may think no one is listening, but God hears you. Let others know you are thankful for His gifts. God loves to listen to you share about how caring, generous, and forgiving He is. We are a living example of God spreading His presence in the world.

There's a quote that's been attributed to everyone from Mahatma Gandhi to Margaret Thatcher that strikes a chord in me. I wish I could hunt down the origin, but the closest I can come is from a man named Frank Outlaw who used to own some grocery stores, but what he said isn't quite as resonant as the original quote I found. Regardless of who said it or when, I'm including it here because I think it might strike a chord with you too:

Keep your thoughts positive because your thoughts become your words.

Keep your words positive because your words become your behavior.

Keep your behavior positive because your behavior becomes your habits.

Keep your habits positive because your habits become your values.

Keep your values positive because your values become your destiny.

Though the origin remains unclear, for our purposes, I want you to know that God wants you to use it in your life as a way for Him to improve your circumstances. He wants to help you get the life He wants for you. The point of the quote is that this all starts with you.

It starts with your positive thoughts and perceptions about life. God's gifts await you! With your God Box, the sky is the limit to where you can be tomorrow, next week, or next year. Surround yourself with positive people and focus on life's goodness. Be a friend and listen to those who need a shoulder to cry on, but do not let them dwell too long on their problems. Help them see the potential beauty of their situation.

I never thought I'd marry again; I can't imagine not being married to my wonderful wife, Christie. I never thought I'd talk to my daughter again; I not only talk with Monique, but see her and my grandson and share in things like working on this book. I thought Christmas only came once a year; I know I can capture that magic any day I want.

I thought life sucked.

Boy, was I wrong. What I needed was an internal change to my attitude, my thoughts and perceptions, my willingness to accept that I deserve to love and be loved.

You do too.

Stand tall, shoulders back, head up, and face life with a smile. Keep your thoughts on the good and grace God has for you, and your life will change in ways you could never imagine. If God created heaven and earth, imagine what He can create in your life! Watch what God has in store for you—it's coming faster than the speed of sound!

If you think this all sounds impossible, then it's pen to paper time for you. Write down "my attitude" or something that best captures why your frame of mind isn't quite right, and give it to God and your God Box.

One last time—think of yourself as a child of the King of Kings, then act like it. Do it with grace and humility, and God's favor will shine through. It all starts with your thoughts and perceptions. Be grateful to God, use your God Box, and enhance your life. If you do that, life won't suck anymore. In fact, maybe your dreams will all come true.

Making Dreams Come True

I love to watch all kinds of sports. I enjoy watching good scary movies. I watch way too much television. When I was a teenager, and throughout my life, my stepfather, Lawrence Garcia, gave me sound advice and excellent instruction on how to live a rich and productive life. I did not always follow it; I rebelled against his advice. Since the fog has cleared because of using my God Box and letting God heal me, I now understand what Lawrence was trying to tell me.

My stepdad treated my mom like a queen—quite differently from the way my biological dad treated her—and I will always love Lawrence unconditionally for that. My stepdad made sure all his wife's wants and needs were met. Both of his parents died when he was just five years old. He told me memories of how poor he and his brothers were when he was little. He shared he was embarrassed to wear the same dirty clothes to school every day, and they only ate pinto bean sandwiches for lunch. His dream was to become an architect. Despite being poor, having no parents, and being a less-than-average student, he achieved his goal. He made his dreams come true by working hard and trusting in God. He used his time to attend school, study, and work to support himself. Meanwhile, his friends were making their heroes' dreams come true instead of their own.

As I said, I love to watch sports. My favorite is football. I'm a big Denver Broncos fan. At one time, I didn't care who was playing—I would start watching college football early Saturday morning, then watch the pros on Sunday for ten hours. My obsession would not end until the last game was played Monday night. And indeed, I was *obsessed* with football. I loved the action. I revered my heroes in the game like they were gods.

My goal as a child was to play professional football. It didn't matter that I was too small, slow, and dropped out of high school. I wanted to be like my heroes; I wanted fame and fortune. To me, they were superstars. I bought their gear and proudly wore my favorite players' numbers on my chest.

One day, my stepdad gave me advice that didn't make sense, at least not then. He said I was making other people's dreams come true—those football players and actors that I watched all day. He suggested that instead of making their dreams come true, why didn't I use that time and energy on my own?

I was surprised by what he was telling me. I didn't draft the players into the pros; their hard work and luck got them there. I didn't cast Brad Pitt in *Legends of the Fall* and make him famous. How did I have any part in making their dreams come true?

I mulled it over. Would Serena or Vanessa Williams strive to be the best tennis players in the world for only the love of the game? I suspect many of our heroes wouldn't strive for greatness if it weren't for their fame, fortune, and fans. We make their dreams come true. We pay twenty dollars to see them in a movie, hundreds of dollars for a Broadway play, or thousands to travel to a live football game. We buy their merchandise and pay for their sponsors by watching commercials on TV. The reason athletes aspire to play sports is, of course, for the love of the game. But another powerful draw is the possibility of earning millions of dollars and the thrill of thousands of fans screaming for them to make the winning touchdown or homerun. Who wouldn't love that kind of admiration and praise? Not to mention the paycheck that can come with them.

Lawrence wasn't telling me to stop watching football or movies. He was trying to get me to see how I spent so much time and energy making other people's hopes and dreams come true while neglecting my own. I love football to this day, and I still celebrate my heroes; they have worked hard to get to where they are and they deserve our applause and cheers. I love to see Serena ace a serve on the tennis court or see a great play on the football field. Whether the Broncos win or lose no longer affects the rest of my life the way it used to. I no longer obsess over the game. I pick one to watch, enjoy the moment, and move on to the next thing in my life (truthfully, I've watched a few games while authoring this book—yes, I can walk and chew gum at the same time…usually, anyways).

Today, I make my dreams come true. You and I are meant to do amazing things. I dream of spreading the word about God to different people, to tell them how God turned a man addicted to meth and Captain Morgan's Rum, was selfish and self-centered, homeless and mentally and emotionally sick, into a healthier man who thrills at helping people, lives in a warm home with a beautiful wife, has reconnected with his precious daughter and grandson, abides the law of the land, surrounds himself with friends, and who loves God. I want to share with people this transformation.

I want to share my spiritual journey so more people can understand the growth God has in store for them. The God of my understanding wants me to speak to those who hold different beliefs and doctrines and let them know that God loves them, no matter by what name they call Him or what house of worship they enter. My God wants me to help others do amazing things. And I will not get there by watching five movies in a row or sitting in front of the TV watching football every weekend from when I wake up to when I go to bed.

Of course, it's okay to support sports—it's fun and exciting and gives us a sense of community! But also make sure you leave enough time to manifest your hopes and dreams each day. Don't obsess about your heroes. Don't let Hollywood or television control your life. You hold the remote control in your hand—hit the power button, turn it off, and get to work on your destiny. Then share with others what God is doing in your life.

What's your dream? Do you have an ideal job in mind? Go big with your goals and watch God's supernatural powers open doors like no man or woman can. You might have to do some work to make it happen. But you can't do the job if you are too busy making others' dreams come true by watching them perform on the big screen or on the field.

Do you want to be an actor, musician, entertainer, or author? Do you like to share the good news of your religion with others? What is your dream job? Do you want to start a new business or move on to a new adventure? God will give you the strength to do what you thought possible. And the possibilities are endless. Make sure you devote enough time each day to make things happen.

You have learned how to make a God Box. I have given examples of how trusting God and using a God Box can change your life. I've clued you in that you might have to do some work. Now, I tell you this: The path of least resistance is giving it to God and your God Box and allowing Him to guide you to fulfill your dream.

I know I keep using myself as an example, but if God can take a guy like me, who once lived on the streets and was mentally ill as well as physically and emotionally broken, and turn him into an inspirational writer, a loving husband, and a trusted father—imagine what He can do for you right now. I'm a guy who needs help to spell or create a proper sentence, and yet here I am, authoring a book.

Start now! Pen to paper time: Set aside this book for a moment, write down one of your dreams on paper, and put it in your God Box.

Did you do it? Don't worry… I'll wait…

Good for you! Get ready to have miracles materialize in your life. Yes, you might have to work or learn a new trade. To be a chef, it could be you have to attend culinary school and learn how to properly mince onions. You're not likely to become a culinary powerhouse by sitting on the couch, eating chips, and watching your favorite TV chef make her world-famous shrimp gumbo.

Start now and get busy making your dreams come true. Your kids, family, and friends will be so proud of you. You will feel good about yourself. If you dream about spending more time with your family or friends, call them up and invite them to lunch or to go for a walk. Get out and enjoy life. Will you wish you watched more TV at the end of your life? I doubt it. You will wish you had spent more time with loved ones. I know this one all too well, as you will learn in an upcoming chapter.

If it's love you dream about, put yourself out there (remember my mother's friend, Mary). Join a singles group, a book club, or a hiking group. Tell your friends you're looking for love—they might know someone who would be a good fit for you. Love is complicated, but it's also quite simple—it takes two. So, go out there and find your Prince Charming or Lady Godiva or whoever it is that makes you feel more complete. Chances are, they're looking for you too.

After all, my mother was with my biological father, but then she found her real love, my stepfather.

Speaking of Lawrence, he provided another piece of wisdom that God wants me to share with you. I was arguing with Mom over some advice she shared with me that I didn't want to hear. I got mad like an idiot and stomped to another room to cool off. Lawrence came to me and said, "Your mom may not always be right, but without question, she is the one person who has your best interest at heart. Your mom doesn't want to see you get hurt. She has only good intentions for you. She will never intentionally lead you down the wrong path."

He was right. My mom always led me down the right path. She always had my best interest at heart. She loved me, and she loved me throughout her life. She always put her children's needs before hers, even when we didn't deserve it. She was a great mom, even when we couldn't see it.

I look at the God of my understanding in the same light. God will never lead us down the wrong path. His is the path of least resistance. God does not want us to suffer or go through pain. We must trust God to make the best decisions for us.

Sometimes it might look wrong to us, but God knows what He's doing. Like my mom, God has our best interests at heart. So, trust that intuitive thought that comes to you. When God says "Jump," by all means, jump! When God prompts you to make that phone call, make it. We never know what's in store for us. God's grace and blessings have snowballed in my life, gaining momentum and size. I trusted God and placed my dreams in His hands through the God Box.

We take advice from people we don't know and who probably don't really care about us. If Dr. Phil were not an expert in his field, do you think people would care what he says about mental health issues? Probably not. You don't call a plumber if you're having a heart attack. We turn to experts when we're dealing with a problem we don't know how to handle. Why not go to the God of ultimate wisdom when you need guidance with things only God can oversee? He will guide us with love. He has no ulterior motive; He's not trying to make a buck. He has no hidden agenda behind His gifts and guidance other than to enrich your life and draw you nearer to Him.

Don't get me wrong—I have trusted friends I can bounce ideas off. Every Oprah Winfrey should have their Gale King. Get their advice, and then filter it through God. You may wonder, *How do I do that?* Here's what I do: I ask myself, "Would a judge, my mom, my wife, and my spiritual advisor approve of what I'm thinking of doing?" If the answer is "No," then God would not approve either. If even one of those people doubts my actions, thoughts, or motives, I need to reconsider my plans. I suggest you find four people in your life with your best interest at heart and listen to their consensus until you learn to hear God's voice. Today I know through an intuitive thought or gut feeling when I'm not doing what I should be, and sometimes I flat out hear God say, "Mark, I don't think so."

I once heard someone say that the five people we spend time with most are the ones who shape our character. We learn behavior and actions through others. Is the God of your understanding in your top five? If He isn't, then put Him there. Spend more time with Him, even if you can't quite hear Him yet. You will. God has the answers, and His guidance is perfect. Discover what works best for you to communicate with your Higher Power.

I start my day with my Higher Power and suggest you do the same. Remember to trust in God and not in the world (and especially not in TV, as much as we may love it). Follow the promptings of God to act, and don't be swayed by outside influences. Remember that we do not necessarily need what our minds want. Let God's wisdom guide you, and graciously accept His favor and blessings. Make your dream come true by trusting in God and a God Box.

God's Gifts vs. God's Grace

Folks, it's soul-searching time. Time to look within and ask some deep questions. Our journey is about to come to an end for some of you. I know there are still a couple of chapters left in this book, but you're not required to read them. If you think you've gotten all you need to know out of this little book, you can stop reading now.

This isn't a gimmick to get you to read the rest of the book. It's time to contemplate what you want out of life. The choice you make may be life-changing, no matter which path you choose to follow. What do you want out of your God Box? Gifts and glory? That's fine; God has those material things waiting for you. He wants to give you all that your heart desires. Or instead, do you seek inner peace and the resilience to manage whatever life throws you? If so, read on—the rest of the book is designed specifically for you. If you, like me, want to enjoy life like we never thought possible, please keep reading. Do you desire to change from the inside out? Read this book to the end and you won't regret it.

If you have no desire to transform and are focused on getting your day-to-day needs met, I understand. Please continue to use your God Box; fill it up with the people, places, and things you want or need. Continue to ask for God's intervention in your life and the lives of your loved ones. Let God enlarge your territory in the material realm. And please, remember to share your stories of the gifts that God has given you. Thanks for reading this far.

But do read on if you want to deepen your relationship with the God of your understanding. Peace, love, and joy will be your rewards.

So, you see, the choice is yours: Are you content with receiving God's gifts? Or do you want to go further and receive God's grace? Even if it means sacrificing some material things?

Now a message from God:

I am called many names by many people. I want to tell you that I am the God of your understanding. I wish all would be happy, loving, and at peace with one another. I want you to have all your needs met; I want to give you all the good things your heart desires. I want you to feel the love I have for each of you. I ask that all of you take care of each other and treat others as you would love to be treated yourself. Stop fighting in My name; there is no need for separation between you. Be good and be safe on your journey through life.

A question stands before you: Is it material goods that make a man or woman, or is it their character? You demonstrate your character in how you feel about, act upon, and share those things I have given you. If you trust Me, I will provide you with what you need and want. I want you to have peace of mind and serenity. I want you to have all the good things you want. I would not be a good Father if I did not grant My children some things that will enhance life, nor would I be a good Father if I gave all things to you regardless of whether or not they are harmful. I have used Mark to share what I hope for you in your life.

If you read on, you will understand why there are no guarantees on what you will get from Me. The question that I face when you make a request is whether it will genuinely make you happy. Will it be in your best interest to receive this thing? Until you read the last chapters, you might not understand what I am saying now. The choice is yours to read on or to stop reading. I will grant many things to people who read up to this turning point. If you choose to read on, then in the future, when you ask My favor, I will determine what is best for you, a gift, or My grace.

My children, enjoy all the blessings about to come your way.

Read on and receive the blessings of My grace or stop here and receive my gifts.

The following chapters will change you in ways you never thought possible. They are about attaining inner peace. They are about altering the way you look at life. It is a change and a peace that leaves you expecting nothing in return. God has assured me He has a better life for you. I do not know how it will be better; I know that it will get better if you turn it over to God and your God Box.

From here on out, I cannot make any guarantees about the things you will get, but I can guarantee that you will find something that you didn't even realize was missing from your life. Read on and unlock the key to what the God Box was truly designed for—not gifts, but grace.

The Art of Forgiveness

You decided to read on—congratulations!

You are going to better understand the deeper meaning of the God Box. I hope you desire a life full of joy and happiness. I hope you seek peace of mind no matter what life hands you. Continuing to delve more deeply into the art of the God Box will bring you joy, peace, and a sense of well-being in ways you could never imagine.

So, why the big secret? What was the big deal about continuing to read or stopping at the previous chapter? At this juncture, you decided whether you wanted the God of your understanding to provide your material desires or to teach you to be content with what you have, whether you wanted Him to change the circumstances in your life so you'd feel more comfortable or to give you serenity no matter what the circumstances. God can provide you with fish so you can eat today, or He can teach you how to fish so you'll be able to eat every day. It's all a question of what you want out of life and how you look at life in general. God can teach us to be happy, loving, and caring no matter our situation or the outcome. You have chosen wisely.

The true meaning of the God Box starts with gaining a new perspective. Read these last two chapters and see what Heaven on Earth looks like.

The God Box was not invented by some guy like me trying to get some stuff. The lineage I am aware of was passed down to help folks deal with addictions they couldn't overcome and issues they needed God's help with. I know that material things and supernatural healings were not even a thought at the time.

The original intent was to help people find comfort in situations that didn't feel good and to cope with their difficulties in healthier ways. It was an aid in learning to turn over to God those matters that required His intervention.

I have shared with you what the God Box has given me. I have talked with others; they claim it has worked for them. Since I started this process and began educating others about a God Box, everyone has been willing to try it. And all but one, to this day, have seen something positive and good come out of the simple act of using their God Box. The remaining holdout has seen progress and told me that just writing down her children's names and putting them in her God Box was a big step. As someone who knows her, I know that it was. She has been going through a whole lot with her marriage and her children, and though she holds onto her anger at times, those of us who know her have observed a change in her. She seems calmer, more at peace with the situation than she did before, but she's early in her journey yet.

To put it bluntly, and I'm sure this is not much a surprise if you pay attention to chapter titles, it's time to talk about the importance of forgiveness. I know very little about all the religions and spiritual principles the people of the world follow. I only know what God and others have shown and given me. I have learned that forgiveness is one of the cornerstones of most organized religions, movements, and faiths. The God of my understanding wants a whole chapter dedicated to this and this subject alone. I'm not going to argue. There will be no sales pitches in this chapter. Will you and I continue to get material things from using the God Box? There's a strong possibility, but honestly, that's between you and your God. My God says that if you master the art of turning things over to Him through your God Box and for the highest good for all, most of the other stuff will no longer matter to you.

Enough about stuff and things and the tangible. God wants me to take this seriously and show you how to look at the world through new eyes by trusting God and using your God Box. This chapter is about shifting your perspective, seeing situations in a different light, and responding to them in caring and understanding ways. Maybe it isn't as simple as getting a new pair of eyes, but most of us can grasp the concept of a new set of glasses to correct our vision. That's what I'm really talking about here. I want you to slip on a new pair of shades with corrective lenses. Those lenses will help you see the world with more compassion, understanding, and love. You might still have your original peepers, but that doesn't mean you can't force yourself to put on your new glasses every morning to try to see the world in a better light.

There is a saying that the eyes are the window to the soul. How do you look at the world? Do you see the divisions and ask yourself, *What can I do to help resolve these issues peacefully and with compassion?* It can be difficult—trust me, I know—but it's important to ask yourself this question. As a matter of fact, I'm going to ask you some more questions and I want you to really think on them; don't answer instantly. Really think about conversations and opportunities and answer them honestly:

Do you bring equanimity and compromise to your political party differences?

- Do you strive for harmony between the races of humanity?
- Do you accept other religions and spiritual beliefs with curiosity and joy?
- Do you invite those different from you to break bread with you?
- Can you forgive those who have wronged you?

As big as all those questions are, that last one might be the most important. I know many of you are saying to yourself, "I've never committed violence. I have no ill will towards anyone. I'm a good person." That's what most people think about themselves, but if that were entirely true, we wouldn't have the problems we have today. People are going hungry and sleeping on streets, children are afraid to go to school and parents are afraid to send them, and in too many countries, many are being persecuted and killed for their race, religion, and political views. The list is endless of the suffering and discord in our world. We start to change things when we look at humanity with compassion and love. We need to forgive those around us.

It's difficult, but it's important that you release the negative thoughts and emotions that now control your life. It's essential to forgive those people who have hurt you in the past. It even matters if you can think of that irritating coworker as an ally instead of a hindrance. This all goes back to simple tenets we learn as children, like the aforementioned Golden Rule or the old standard about "love thy neighbor," but while those things may have seemed simple when we were young, as we grow older and life becomes more complicated, we tend to think that these basic morals should also become more complicated. But I disagree. I say that we should more often try looking at others through a lens of compassion, love, understanding, and forgiveness. Even when it's tough, we must attempt this, or things are bound to get worse.

This chapter is more serious; it addresses some real and painful issues, but I hope by the end, you will see what true forgiveness looks like. I hope you will see how God can give you inner peace when you trust Him in all things. It may teach us all to look through that all-important compassionate and forgiving lens. And here comes the toughest part of this book for me to write…

My mom, Bea Ann, married my dad, Henry, when she was fourteen and he was twenty-one. They went on to have three children, my two older brothers and me. From what I've been told, Mom had it rough from the start. My dad beat her and abused her verbally, mentally, and emotionally. He was, without question, a violent man. I don't even want to remember these times; I don't want to relive that pain. But for the highest good of all, I will. You see, this is my story of how my dad used to beat the hell out of the person who gave me life. Years later, it still stings to talk about it. But it doesn't hurt the way it used to because I look at it through my glasses of compassion, love, understanding, and forgiveness; I have given it to God and my God Box.

When I was a child, my dad would get drunk and start accusing my mom of being a whore and a slut. My mom was a loving and faithful wife to him. They were ridiculous accusations, and I still don't understand how he ever dared to make them. But he was just getting started. He would throw food in her face and break the furniture. I remember her body covered in different shades of bruise—black and blue, purple and yellow. The worst was hearing her scream for help. I'm sorry, Mom. I wish I could have stopped him, but I was just a little boy. I can still hear her crying out for him to stop. I hear the wails of women worldwide ringing in my ears, the anguished cries of the abused. My mom's screams cut deep and broke my heart.

For many years, my mom suffered the pain and agony of abuse. She finally had enough and filed for divorce when I was seven or eight. I thought the violence was over and done with, but I was wrong. My dad stalked, harassed, and assaulted my mom many times until the divorce was finalized. I remember us huddled in fear as my dad broke down the door to get to her.

I don't know if that actually happened or if it's the remnant of some nightmare, but it's one of those memories in my gut and the terror I felt was very real. I constantly worried for Mom—my dad had lost control. A bad situation was turning into a living nightmare; I know that much is true.

I was forced to visit with my dad during the divorce. I shouldn't say forced because he was my dad, and I did love him even though I was afraid. He was a sick man in need of help. One night in particular, my dad picked me up to spend the night with him. He took me to a fast-food restaurant, and while we waited, he asked, "What's your whore-mother doing?"

Naïve and only seven years old, I answered him truthfully and said she was getting ready to go on a date. That was a huge mistake. A bomb exploded inside of my dad. I saw the devil himself materialize right before my eyes. Of course, it wasn't actually the devil—it was my father, Henry Martinez, misusing his free will. My God defines evil as the misuse of free will, and in that moment, I saw pure evil. My dad was mad as hell, and he was going to find my mom and that son of a bitch she was on a date with and make sure they both knew that Bea Ann was his wife and no one's date.

I was immediately interrogated. He wanted to know when, where, and who she was with. I had no clue and couldn't answer his questions. I was scared and afraid of what my dad would do. He formulated a plan; he would watch our house and wait for Mom and her date to return. My dad was a stalker waiting for his prey with his young son, but he was too messed up in his own fury to recognize how twisted the situation he created was. We waited down the street, hiding in a car he borrowed from a friend so she wouldn't recognize it. He was the lion, the king of the jungle, and I was his cub. Together, he waited to pounce on the unsuspecting victims as I trembled at what he might be trying to teach me.

My mom and her date drove up and parked in a driveway—not at our house, but at my aunt and uncle's, five houses down. Dad sprang into action, pulled his car forward to block the driveway, and then jumped out like a man possessed. My mom leapt from her date's car and dashed for my aunt and uncle's door. I don't know why my mom went there in the first place, but I know she was trying to get to safety at that point. My dad caught Mom by her hair and dragged her in front of the other man's car, where he hit her repeatedly in the face. He bellowed at Mom's date to get out of the car so he could beat his ass, too, but the man just cowered in his vehicle. I held it against him for years, but now I realize he was not willing to risk his life to save a woman he hardly knew in a situation that he probably couldn't understand quickly enough.

I exited the car, shouting at my dad to stop hurting my mom. He was out of control and no longer present. My mom's bloody face went blank, and then her body went limp. Dad's face went from rage to zero emotion. Mom was unconscious.

My father was insane.

My aunt and uncle ran out of their house, screaming at my dad to stop before he killed her. He snapped out of the evil spell he was under and dropped my mom on the sidewalk. I can still hear the sound of her skull striking the concrete. I grabbed her hand and tried to hold on to her as Dad dragged me away. Dad snatched me up and threw me into his car. My aunt and uncle begged him not to kidnap me.

I don't know how much time passed, whether it was hours or days. The next thing I remember is that I was in a house or a hotel, and my dad was on the phone with the police saying he would surrender. The cops came to the door, and my dad opened it like he was greeting a door-to-door salesman. They put him in handcuffs and placed him under arrest. I was so distraught that I cried for the man who had beaten my mother to a bloody pulp. I didn't want my dad to leave me. As it was, he only spent a few weeks behind bars. Times were different then. He only got a slap on the wrist for beating a woman unconscious in front of their shared child.

I don't know how long my mom was in the hospital. I think she was in a coma. I could ask my aunt and uncle, but I don't want to know. My mom is no longer alive, and I would never have asked her to relive that time. I remember after she left the hospital, she and I sat in one of those rounded booths at a diner like IHOP or Denny's. I was sitting so close to her that you couldn't peel me off with a potato knife. She told me I could get whatever I wanted to eat, even a malt. *A malt!* I still consider this the second-best day in my life after the birth of my daughter. It felt heavenly to hold on to my dear mother after fearing that I might lose her forever.

I wish I could tell you that was the last time Mom had to deal with my dad, but it wasn't. For the next five or six years, she put up with his calls and harassment.

Nothing I can say can ever justify what my dad did. Like I said, times were different back then. Society and the law shrugged off spousal abuse as a private issue. In the United States, things have changed somewhat, but from what I can tell worldwide, not at all. Men continue to abuse women and children. Women abuse other women, men, and children. Men beat other men in the context of domestic abuse. Abuse is abuse, no matter who the victim or the perpetrator might be. It is a worldwide crisis that needs to be addressed. It cuts across all genders, races, religions, and economic strata. But you know what? Change starts with you and me.

I know now that I need to be the change I want to see. I can't force the whole world to change, but I can certainly change the world around me. And so can you. If we each change our little circle and stand together, linking all our circles, we have the ability to change this entire planet of Earth. I believe in us! I believe person by person that worldwide change is possible! And so should you, especially now that you know the power of a God Box.

God and my God Box have taught me to be the man God has always wanted me to be. God does want us to have material things, but most of all, God wants us to have peace of mind, body, and spirit. If you had the choice between giving your child a new toy and providing them a lifetime of peace and serenity, which would you choose for them as a good parent? God is the ultimate parent and wants to give you the best of gifts. He will care for your material needs but wants you to have so much more. He wants you to experience peace and joy, love and acceptance, and an amazing life! God wants to teach us how to be happy whether or not we get our material desires fulfilled. God gives me strength and guidance in all aspects of my life. Now, I want a life filled with joy and free from worry and fear.

If we want the life God wants for us, we must learn to forgive those who wronged us. If we want peace of mind, we must forgive those who have hurt us emotionally, physically, or mentally. That doesn't mean we must befriend and hang out with them. We never even have to see that person, place, or thing that harmed us ever again. We need only to let it go and let God take care of things out of our control. On my own, I could never summon the will to forgive my dad for what he did. But God, through that Voodoo He does so well, gave me His Blessing, the power of forgiveness even when I wasn't seeking it. I didn't even know it was happening inside me.

Letting go was something I couldn't achieve on my own. I tried counseling and therapy, drugs and alcohol, church, books, and many other things to eliminate the hatred and vengeance I carried. None of it worked. The drugs and alcohol temporarily masked the hurt and torment I felt, but the bad feelings always returned. I had to turn it over to the care of God because only He could relieve me of that hurt and pain. Therapy is excellent, and I recommend you seek it if it is available to you. For me, medication, therapy, and praying were a good start. Still, the healing didn't occur until I let go and let God take over. I needed to be free from anger, hate, and animosity towards all to create a place of serenity and peace. I demonstrated my commitment to getting well mentally, emotionally, and spiritually by writing it all down and putting it in my God Box.

If I had never forgiven my dad, my daughter would have missed out on a relationship she absolutely loved. Seeing my dad and Monique spending time together was priceless. Nothing in the material world could have ever replaced the time she spent and all that she learned and experienced with her Grandpa Martinez. If I had clung to my hurt and angry feelings for my dad, I would have kept the cycle of hatred and anger alive for the next generation and denied my child the joy she experienced. Somehow, my dad, who was absolutely horrendous as a father and husband, became the most incredible, fantastic, excellent grandfather I've ever seen. He loved Monique and took care of her all the time. My daughter never had to see my dad's angry, ugly side. She was his only grandchild, and she loved him unconditionally. He responded to the love he received from her by giving her love in return, fully and abundantly. God transformed that man in ways I could never have imagined. Why did God choose to change him? Like most things when it comes to Him and how He works, I don't know. I'm just grateful He did. My dad quit drinking, and by God's grace, he became a good man.

But what about my mom, Bea Ann? How could she ever forgive a man who brutalized her like he did? For Mom, it was easy; she looked at him through the lens of compassion and forgiveness I keep going on about. She saw him as a sick man who needed help. She felt sorry for him and tried to help him through the years, no doubt praying for him unceasingly. She told me not to hate my father; she said he was a sick man, not an evil or bad man. When there were family gatherings like weddings and other functions, they had to be in the same room. My mom always invited him to sit with her and my stepdad, Lawrence. My mom showed him love. She had compassion for a man she could easily have hated. She was a marvel of forgiveness.

Later in life, my mom literally killed my dad with love. Remember that from the beginning? Truly, she killed him with love!

My dad had a heart attack and was in a coma for a few weeks. It must've been karma for what he did to her, but that's not for me to say. He came out of the coma and was on the mend. He spent two more months in the hospital recuperating. He was doing well, so they transferred him to a rehab center. Monique and I went to visit my dad and ensure he was comfortable. Mom called and asked if we wanted to go to lunch with her. We said sure, but it'd be a little while because we were visiting Dad. She decided to join us. Mom arrived, and Dad was lying on his bed conscious, alert, and well. He was smiling from ear to ear because the three people who loved him most were there. Yes, unbelievable as it might seem, my mom still loved him.

Dad couldn't talk very well due to complications from having had all those tubes down his throat for months. That was okay. My mom could do all the talking. After a few minutes of "How are you feeling, Henry?" and other such small talk, the air in the room suddenly got a different vibe. Mom got serious. My daughter and I fell silent. The room was as eerily still, and I could feel God's presence. My mom scooted her chair closer to the bed and took my dad's hand. Looking into his eyes, she said, "Henry, I forgive you for everything you did to me." My dad's eyes teared up, and he started to cry.

Then, my mother did something even more astounding: She leaned over and kissed him. She kissed that man—her ex-husband, a man who had abused her regularly, who had made ten years of her life a living hell, who had once beaten her into a coma—she kissed him right on the lips. Then she leaned back and told him that she loved him and always had. She didn't say anything more. She didn't remind him of all the pain he had caused her and their family.

She didn't elaborate on what her kiss or forgiveness meant. A simple kiss on the lips and an I love you were all she needed to express the sincerity of her forgiveness.

There was no need for her to explain that her love was different from what it had been when he came rolling up in his sailor suit to take her to the dance fifty years ago. She loved this man not for his actions but because they had children together. She loved him first and foremost because she knew he was a child of God. She saw him through her own lens of love, compassion, understanding, and forgiveness. And she did just that. Mom forgave him.

My mom, Bea Ann, with her great grandson Jack

Not that she would have phrased it the way I do with the lens. But that's how I think about it—just like a new pair of prescription glasses. Our vision may be warped. Everything may be tinted gray instead of rose. I get it. Some of us don't see the world easily the way God wants us to see it, but God wants us to try on a pair of glasses. They might look old and worn, but they're brand new to you. You can trust they have been used only for good and for God. When you put them on, your whole outlook will change.

When someone cuts you off in traffic, slip on those fancy specs. If anyone talks bad about you, spreads false rumors, stabs you in the back, or lies to your face, see them through the eyes of God's forgiveness, for we are all human beings just trying to get this life right.

My mom's story doesn't end there. If I had not witnessed and participated in what happened next, I wouldn't have believed it myself. My daughter and I were stunned and deeply moved by what Mom had just done. Then, shortly after leaving the rehab to go to lunch, I got a call on my cell phone. The rehab center called to tell me that my dad passed away minutes after we left. He went peacefully, knowing he was loved and forgiven by three generations of his family. My mom killed my dad that day with love. I know my dad is in Heaven despite his past misdeeds. My God is a God of forgiveness, and my parents followed this same God.

If forgiveness can kill a man's body (or set him free of it, as it were), imagine what lack of forgiveness does physically. Carrying around that kind of anger and resentment eats us alive, as does carrying the shame and guilt of not seeking forgiveness for what we have done. My dad fought off death through a heart attack, coma, strokes, and God knows what else, just to stay alive long enough to be killed by love. When all was said and done, the act of being forgiven broke his chains in this life to pass on to the next. If that doesn't demonstrate the power of forgiveness, I don't know what will.

Forgiveness can free you from so many burdens, not only in receiving it but by offering it. Do you have to kiss everyone you forgive? Of course not—I promise I'm not telling you to go on a smooching frenzy. But God will reveal what you need to do through an intuitive thought or the suggestions of others.

You know what to do. Write down the person or situation you need to forgive and put it in your God Box, then allow God to bless you with His favor and grace. Feel His presence around and within you like I and many others have felt when we've let go of the hurts and atrocities of the past. I was sexually abused by a family member when I was young. If my mom can forgive her abusive ex-husband, I, too, can forgive those who have hurt me. I have forgiven the man who molested me, and I mean it. I'm not going to carry that awfulness with me another day. Pain runs deep, and emotional wounds feel like they'll never heal. I put that sick man in my God Box, then let go and allowed God to heal me. I am free to walk this earth without animosity towards that man. He had to live with what he did. Today, I refuse to give anyone the power to control how I think or feel; in order to take back my power, I had to forgive that man.

God has given me stuff you will read about in the next chapter, but the real gift He has given me is how to deal with myself. He has shown me how to resolve those issues that used to make me feel uncomfortable and act out. I no longer think about the things that used to keep me all night. God has given me supernatural powers of my own. Some things no longer exist for me, like the compulsion to drink and do drugs to forget my thoughts and numb my feelings. I now have God-given supernatural powers to heal myself using my God Box. Nothing had worked for me before to remove the pain and memories of the harm done to me or that I had inflicted on others. God has the power to do all this and more. God gave me the ability to live with my trauma. He took away the sting of being harmed and the vengeful thoughts I had carried for so long. God has given me the supernatural power to deal with life on life's terms.

There is power in that Box that awaits you. But you have to want it. You must write down your need for help and turn it over to God. God can send you on a trip to Hawaii and make you feel better for a week, or He can give you supernatural powers to heal yourself daily. This is the start of our new journey with God and our God Boxes. Ask God to provide you with supernatural powers to help you heal from all the things that have been done to you. Learn to look at your fellows through the glasses of love, compassion, understanding, and forgiveness. As you do so, God will reward you with a peace that surpasses comprehension.

Truth Be Told

Dear reader,

These are the last steps in our journey towards a new and wonderful life.

Cancer took my mother's life like it has so many others. My mom was in her seventies when she died. I wish I could tell you that God and my God Box saved her life. I can't. Truth be told, I didn't know what a God Box was at the time. I can tell you my mom was a spiritual woman who loved God. I'm a lot like my mom, not just in her love for God but in her character defects. She, like me, was a recovering addict. Her two addictions were gambling and alcohol. Gambling, oh, how my mom loved to gamble! When cancer took my mom, she had not stepped foot in a casino in nearly five years, and I'm proud to say she had over thirty-three years of sobriety.

My mother did not die a rich woman. Mom met her second husband after her first failed marriage to my dad. Lawrence was a successful architect who designed and built many buildings and bridges in my home state. He wasn't wealthy, but he made a good living. My mom had a career in cosmetics that afforded her a very comfortable life. My parents, at one time, were bringing in a quarter of a million dollars a year. Then, my stepdad died, and that's when my mom's gambling addiction took over. She spent half a million dollars in her last two years of gambling—she lost it all. Fortunately, a reverse mortgage allowed her to stay in her house.

Mom was proud to be a member of both Alcoholics Anonymous and Gamblers Anonymous. She was a wonderful role model, and she lived to help others. She sponsored and helped many other addicted people to develop a life worth living.

One night, I got a call from Uncle Rick. My mom had been rushed to the emergency room. He told me to get there as soon as possible, that the end was near. I got there as fast as I could. Mom had been sick and in pain for over a year. Now, she was dying. But she was a fighter and held on for dear life.

Days went by. My mom could still speak, so friends and family visited, knowing it would be the last time they saw her alive. She was in painful misery, yet she refused narcotic medication because she wanted to stay lucid. My ex-wife, who my mother loved like her own, sat with my daughter and me through the week as Mom struggled to stay alive. We stayed by her, prayed, and waited for her to pass, as so many have done in the last moments of a loved one's life.

Mom was in so much pain on one particular day that she could hardly catch her breath. One of my mom's dearest friends was visiting (it pains me to admit it, but I can't remember this sweet soul's name), and she sat down beside her, holding Mom's head up so she could drink some cool water and ease her thirst. Then, looking into her eyes, this wonderful friend said to Mom, "Bea, it's okay to let go. Go on to Heaven and be with God." My mom got the saddest look on her face I have ever seen. She looked at her friend, then at me, and said, "I don't want to die because I will miss my children." She spoke from the depths of her heart, and it shattered me.

I cry like a baby every time I recall that moment.

How could she say such a thing? My brothers and I were in and out of hospitals, jails, and psych wards for years, bringing her so much worry and trouble. Was she going to miss us? I felt like a loser for all the time I had wasted on drugs, gambling, and booze. I chased women of every variety, trying to find love and approval, and here I'd had it all along in my mother.

I catch myself thinking, *Come back, Mom! Please, Mother! You and me and Monique will get together again and watch the Oscars like we used to. We can go to lunch, see a movie, sit by the fireplace, and talk about all the movie stars we love and hate. Come back for one more day, and I'll attend church with you. I'll do anything you want! Just give me one more minute to tell you I love you, and I'm sorry I didn't tell you that every day. Mom, come back for one more second so I can hold you. Please, Mom, I love you and miss you with all my heart!* But I know it isn't to be so. As much as I wish and think and hope, some things are out of reach.

Mom asked two things of me before she died: First, she asked that I be by her side when she passed away; second, she wanted me to take care of my two brothers to the best of my ability. I have done both.

That cold February day, my daughter held my mom's left hand, and I held her right when she went to be with God. I held her hand with the same fervor I did that day in the restaurant as a little boy. You couldn't peel me off. I never wanted to let go.

The bittersweet memory of those final moments still cuts me to the bone. As I wipe my eyes with the sleeve of my shirt, let me ask, do you know *why* I'm sharing this with you? Did you notice that my mom's final words weren't about taking care of her stuff, car, jewelry, or house? Her final request to me and God had nothing to do with material possessions. She only wanted more time with her children. She only wanted us to be taken care of, even as she drew her last breaths.

Truth be told, God and my God Box have not given me everything I wanted. I haven't gotten my mom back. The pain of that day still feels like it was yesterday when, in fact, it was over four years ago. Here's another truth to be told: Until last week, I hadn't put my mom's death in my God Box yet. Why in the world didn't I do that? I don't know; maybe I was afraid if I asked God to take away the pain of that loss, I'd forget my mom. Just the other day, God whispered in my ear, "Practice what you preach, Mark."

One thing I've learned is that when God speaks, it's a good idea to follow His suggestion. So I said a prayer, wrote my mom's name on a piece of paper, and put it in my God Box. I took a picture so I could show you that I really did it:

What is God whispering in your ear to put in your God Box? Is He telling you to write down a new car, a better job, more money? Do you think that's what you're going to wish you had more of at the end of your life? When your children or loved ones are at your bedside, and they tell you it's okay to let go, will you tell them you can't let go yet because you will miss your house or your Mustang?

My journey through this little book started as a way for me to show you how to get the things you desired and how I got all kinds of great stuff using a God Box. Through the process, however, I've learned much more about what is important in life, and God has rearranged my priorities. Now, I'm more interested in what I can share with others, like time and love, than what I can get for myself. Can I look through those compassion lenses and find someone who has no friends and become a friend to them? Does the God of my understanding tell me to go out and find more love for myself?

Or does He tell me to go out and share His love with others? If my friend Barbara had refused to listen and act when God told her to find me and help me, none of this, none of my current life, would exist. She saved me! God may have sent her, may have whispered in her ear, but I give credit where credit's due: Barbara saved my life. You can save someone else's life and not even know it just by doing something nice.

As I've told you, I was once a very sick man, mentally and emotionally. There was a day when I headed to the park with one goal in mind; I was going to hang myself. I had a rope, and I planned to loop it around a tree branch, tie a noose, and kill myself. On my way to the park, I decided to wave at the cars going by to see if someone would wave back. I wanted to know if there was anyone who cared enough to wave hello to a stranger. If just one person did, I thought it'd give me enough hope to live just one more day. Car after car went by, and not one person responded. I felt invisible, like a ghost, and if they were going to treat me like a ghost, I might as well become a ghost.

Then a little old lady waved at me! I'm beginning to think God sends angels disguised as little old ladies to save us from ourselves… But that's a thread to follow another time. That simple wave was enough to stop me from killing myself. A single gesture had more impact than that little old lady could ever probably believe, but it's true.

Imagine what saying hello to a stranger or buying lunch for someone down on their luck could do for their life. Think of your fellow humans out there, and be the friend or family just one person desperately needs. If you want love in the world, be the love. You want peace. Create peace for your neighbors. Bring the doughnuts! Be a friend to someone lonely. Please, don't ever force yourself on another person; be respectful of others' boundaries. But don't be afraid to shine your inner light and be an example of goodness in the world.

There are so many people who need love, compassion, and peace. Their lifestyle might not be like yours or mine; they might look or dress differently. They might be fearful or cautious around someone like you because of their history and experience. Nevertheless, it's up to us to show kindness to others. We need to love one another despite our differences. God wants us to be His hands and feet in this world.

You may recall that at the beginning of this book, I said that one of my mantras is to help others do amazing things. My primary purpose isn't to get a yacht or a mansion. My purpose is to help others find what they are looking for. What is yours? You just might need more money. Money can solve a lot of our problems, I know. Or you may want more money to spend on more nifty things (and you know how I like nifty things). If you are alone and have no one to share it with, what good is having all the money in the world? What good are the nifty things? Family and friends are what truly matter.

I have friends from all walks of life. I hang out with judges and police officers, and also with criminals trying to turn their lives around. My friends are fathers, mothers, priests and pastors, wealthy people, and homeless folks. I have more friends in my new life than I ever thought possible—good friends, *real* friends—friends who would visit me in the hospital if I was sick or who call when they haven't seen or heard from me in a few days. I have friends that really care about me and not what I have to offer, and vice versa.

God created us to fellowship with Him and each other as friends and family. God wants families reunited, broken friendships repaired, and lonely hearts to feel welcomed. The principles and concepts of the God Box teach us how to give these issues to God so we don't have to worry, stress, or cry about it. The Art of the God Box is about surrendering to the God of your understanding those things we have trouble letting go of, such as a relationship that needs help starting or ending, or worries about children or loved ones. We all can use spiritual assistance of supernatural proportions every now and then.

God wants you to be happy with who you are and how you look. It's terrible that we allow media and commercials to define how we should look, act, and dress. We end up so dissatisfied, thinking things like, *I'm too short. I'm too tall. I'm too skinny. I'm too big. My teeth aren't white enough. I'm driving the wrong car.* Let God and your God Box define who you are, what you will be, how best to behave, and how to treat others.

It's time for some more truth to be told.

As we near the end of our journey together, I want to make clear a few things. First, you're probably wondering if everyone will get what they want out of their God Box.

I want my mother back. Can my God Box bring her back to life? Of course not. But God has assured me that I will get her back! You see, less than an hour after I put my mother's death and my profound sense of loss in my God Box, God showed me that I would be with my mom when I got to my next destination, which I call Heaven. I will see her, hold her, and feel again like I did that day when I was a child, sitting in that booth at that diner. I had never thought of my mom's death that way, and I really didn't believe that my God Box could help in any way to bring her back. But when I took action and used my God Box, I allowed God to shift my perspective, and I could see that I will indeed be with her again! Now, while editing this chapter, tears do not fill my eyes. Instead, joy fills my heart!

Will you get everything you want? I don't know. It probably depends on what you're asking for and how you're asking for it. You can have peace of mind and serenity if you wish. You can be happy with everything you have right now if that is what you ask of God through your God Box.

Do you remember I told you about the house God provided for me and my wife to live in, all paid for? I've never seen a more beautiful place. It's a double-wide trailer on foundations that must be forty or fifty years old.

Heck, the whole trailer's old. It needs a new paint job. My wife has to get up on the roof at least once a month to repair leaks (I would fix them, but I'm too heavy, and my wife is afraid I'll fall through the roof if I go up there). We need a new swamp cooler—ours blows out rusty, metal flakes because it's ancient. But man, I think my home is beautiful.

The neighborhood we live in is commonly called "the war zone." Violence and homelessness are out of control. But you know what? I hardly notice. I've never felt safer in my entire life. I have never felt more grateful for cool air than when that rusty old swamp cooler pumps out what it can in the summer heat. I've lived in houses that others would say are big and beautiful, but I never loved them as much as I love this old trailer. We may not live in in a palace, but to us, that's exactly what it is. I am so grateful! You wouldn't believe it unless you experienced it yourself. God has taught me to put on his wonderful spectacles and see my house as fit for royalty (which I am, if you recall my mother's words about being the child of the King of Kings).

That car the man bought for us with no strings attached—half the time, the heater and air conditioner don't work. There's a loose wire somewhere under the glove compartment, and my wife has to give it a swift kick to jiggle the connection to get the air blowing. God forbid we hit a bump, and it turns off! The car has nearly 130,000 miles on it, but it runs, and when the heater does work—wow! It's so great to be nice and toasty. I much prefer our car than riding the bus and getting punched by some random sick man. I'll take wonky heating and cooling over that any day. And the best part? I no longer worry about how my wife will get to work each day.

It's all a matter of perspective, and God has taught me that. When I first told you about my house, I'm sure none of you envisioned a double-wide trailer with all sorts of issues planted in the roughest part of town. Do you know why? You saw what you wanted to see and believe in your own mind. I love all the things God gives me. Do you know what the best gift God gave me through using the God Box? He gave me the supernatural power to appreciate whatever I have and whatever I receive. I used to think, *The bigger, the better.* If I had a one-story house, I'd want one with two stories. If I had a nice car, I'd want a better car. All that was in my head was *I, me, more, now, faster, more, more, more—more money, more women, more of this, and more of that!* The things I had were never good enough. Now, through the healing power of the Supreme Being, I love and appreciate what little I do have.

I woke up in my drafty house with my crazy dogs and loving wife at five a.m. to write this final chapter. Though I could've woken up in a prison cell, I am a free man! And I'm free to write the books God directs me to write. God put me on this earth to help others do amazing things, and I love every minute of it, drafty or not.

God wants you to know you can have the same blessings I and countless others have received. Just trust in the God of your understanding and the beauty of a God Box. Peace of mind, spiritual, mental, emotional, and physical healings are possible for every one of you. God wants you to know that you can find love for and from others, as I have. God will restore you to peace and serenity where there once was pain and fear.

God can teach you, as He did me, to ask for those things that are the highest good for all. Do I sneak in a little selfish request now and then? I do. One selfish thing I ask for, as you may recall, is to have enough money to take my whole family to Disney World. All twelve of them! Will God grant me that? I don't know. Remember that savings I mentioned in an earlier chapter? It's up to two thousand dollars, and a coffee can full of change. It's a start. I don't remember ever having a savings account in my life. What a God-given gift from my God Box!

So, you see, I got everything I told you about. They may not look how you expected or how I initially visualized them, but God provided everything I need to be happy. Am I content with where I am right now? Yes. Do I want more out of my life? Certainly. Will this book ever get published? Will I ever get a new Mustang convertible? Will I ever get to see Disney World? I don't know. That's up to God and my use of the God Box. I never trusted God before; now I do. I'm asking you to trust Him too.

Will God save your loved one from the grips of addiction? All I know is that if you trust Him, He will give you a fresh perspective and better tools to deal with it. Will you get the new job you're asking for? You might have to work for it. And in the meantime, God can show you how to enjoy where you are instead of pining for where you are not.

Will you find true love? If you think about it, you already have true love through God. I know you want someone—the right someone—to love and to hold. Be patient, put yourself out there, and say hello to that person God puts in your heart. In the meantime, be sure you love yourself and show God's love to those around you.

Are all those situations you put in your God Box going to be resolved quickly and with a happy ending? Maybe, maybe not. I know that God is real and always has your best interest at heart for the highest good of all.

Look deep into your heart and decide what you need or want to be truly happy. Is it the things of this world, or is it the time spent with friends or family? Focus on those things that will bring you joy.

Use your God Box. Place your God Box on your desk at work where others can see it. Keep one at home where your loved ones can witness your commitment to God. Someday, you might master the art of turning over your life to the care of God, believing in it with your mind, body, and soul. Until then, use your God Box. Share your success stories with others. Tell them about the

God of your understanding and your experiences using the God Box. In this way, you can demonstrate the power of God's love and help them see that God is real and cares about us.

Give God Boxes to others so they can experience what has been given to you. Tell them how to use one and assure them it can work for them, too. I truly believe God has material and spiritual gifts for us all. Enjoy and share with others all that God blesses you with. Keep paying it forward, and God will continually refill your cup. Share the love and share the hope, and God will work through you to make the world a better place for all of us.

I am so grateful for everything I have and for whatever is yet to come. I place each of you in my God Box and wish you well on the incredible, exciting journey of newfound freedom and happiness that awaits you. May God's favor and grace rain down on you from this day forward. I will say goodbye for now until we meet here on Earth or in the hereafter.

Mom, I'll see you then. Save me a corner booth and order me a malt, please.

The Greatest Gift of God

(Postscript)

I hope you find or get whatever you are looking for whether those things are money, property, prestige, love, or a miraculous healing. Was it a new job you were looking for when you first thought of trying a God Box? Was it spiritual healing for a loved one that started you on this journey? Who knows why you picked up this book in the first place? You may need something to kick-start you on the road to happiness. Without question, it was a God thing.

Now that you've read this book, you have more tools to create a life you only dreamed of. There are so many things to learn when it comes to God. But you know what? God has more to teach us about Himself, life, and ourselves. When I started on this project, I thought, *What a concept! I can make a few dollars to show people how to get the material things they want.*

Now I see it was much more than just that. He just keeps on surprising me and He'll do the same for you. Our God Boxes can elevate us in ways I had never thought before. I hope you found out what you really want out of life and have a more meaningful connection to that desire, that you're better to understand where your wants and needs come from. Material things are excellent to have and we all will them to come our way, but they will also go. There's always something bigger, better, brighter. Trends change daily.

Clothes and houses and cars and all those shiny things go in and out of style, wear out and down, break or become obsolete, and get lost or stolen. But love and our connections with others grow richer and deeper over time and make our world extraordinary.

Initially, a God Box was a way for people to take things beyond their control and give them to their Higher Power so they could stop worrying about them. This was a good use of a God Box and helped many addicts and alcoholics on their journey to recovery. Through the evolution of time and practice, I have seen that the God Box can be—no, that's not right—*is* much, much more. It's a method to communicate with God on a new level. It's a way to strengthen your faith. No longer will you wonder if God is listening; you will have proof that He is.

The act of writing down what you want or need from God is vital. You can tell Him you need help for a loved one suffering from addiction or mental illness. You can have your needs met if you ask and are ready to do a little work. Yes, God knows all, but writing it down strengthens our commitment and reminds us that God is in control.

By now, your God Box should be full of requests. Some requests you may have already seen come to fruition, and others God is still working on behind the scenes. For those of you who are already in full swing using a God Box, I am sure miracles are appearing in your lives like you never imagined. Don't forget that some of those requests will require a little work. Not everything you get will be due to divine intervention or supernatural healing. If you have a loved one addicted to alcohol who you have placed in your God Box, take them to a meeting of Alcoholics Anonymous—that might be where their miracle awaits them. I don't know when, why, or how God will reveal His plan for you. Just be ready to jump when God says, "Jump!"

I suggest taking time to meditate so you can listen for God's guidance on your next course of action. It may come through an intuitive thought, or you may hear God's voice. God speaks through others, so pay attention to those seemingly chance encounters. Finally, God will never make you beg for or chase after His gifts. Let go and let God.

God has so much in store for you, but you must want it and be willing to take action. You take action when you write what you want and put it in your God Box, then let it go. The act of letting go of your worry or obsession jumpstarts the miracle. I don't know how that works—it just does.

If you were looking for a sign from God to do something to change the way you live, well, here it is. This book is the sign you've been waiting for! Now you have no excuse but to start trusting God. Follow G.O.D. (Good Orderly Direction) and do what God asks of you. God is in control now, and who better to run the show of your life than He who gave you life. You wouldn't go to an electrician to get your teeth worked on, would you? So why put your life into the hands of anyone other than the One who breathed life into you? Don't wait until all else has failed. Give it to God from the start, no matter what it is you seek. It all starts now. No matter the successes or failures in your past, it all starts with a blank slate in the eyes of God.

With God as your source, you have unlimited resources. What will you do with that kind of power? If someone were to make a movie of your life from this day forward, what superpower would they say you possessed? They would say of me, "Mark's superpower is helping others do amazing things."

Am I perfect? No, I'm not. Will I make mistakes? Without question, and so will you. The thing about making mistakes is what we do with it afterward. Do we continue to make the same mistake or learn from it and correct course? Do you know the best thing about not being a saint? There's always room for improvement.

God doesn't expect us to be perfect. Some of our requests will be selfish, and that's okay. We're learning. Realize that God will do what is best for the highest good of all. The highest good for all of mankind, not the highest good for just me or you.

When we demonstrate God's love and goodness to others, it enlarges His presence in the world and is of the highest good for all. Is getting a bigger house or more money for the highest good? It can be if you give all the credit to the God of your understanding. Introduce others to the concept of a God Box and let them know they can connect to God themselves.

Will there be tough times in your future? Probably—no one goes through life without troubles and tribulations—but now you have a God and a God Box you can put your trust in. You will discover a new way of looking at and handling those situations that used to seem so unfair. When life throws you lemons, don't just make lemonade; give the lemons to God and watch what He does with them!

Life is so much better when God is in control. Not only am I free from addiction and mental illness, but I also no longer worry about things that used to baffle me. God has given me a new way to look at everything, and now I can enjoy life as God intended. If God can take a thug like me off the streets and completely turn me around, imagine what He can do for you!

I have shared much with you about myself and my family. I want to tell you one more story before we part ways.

Like I said, my mom was diagnosed with cancer. She was going through chemo, and I was living with her and doing my best to help her through the long days and nights. She had very little money; remember, during her gambling addiction, she had spent all the money she and my stepfather had saved for retirement. It was summer, and it was a hot one. We live in the southwestern United States, and summers in the desert are sweltering. The air conditioner didn't work. We needed a new one, but it would cost at least $16,000 to buy one and get it installed. We didn't have that kind of money, so we did our best.

Upstairs or downstairs, it was hot as hell. It was uncomfortable, but it was home, and we had nowhere else to live. One day, I went to meet some friends at a twelve-step meeting. I turned off my phone for an hour to avoid disturbing the group. I always kept my phone on in case my mom needed to get a hold of me, except for the hour that I was in a meeting. When the meeting ended that day, I turned my phone back on, and there were multiple text messages and voicemails from Mom. Swallowing my fear, I called her back the second my phone was up and running. She said she called because the heater had come on in the house. I thought, *That sure is strange, since it's ninety degrees outside.* She said the heater had come on by itself and swore she never touched it. After it started running, she tried to get it to turn off, but to no avail. My mom had lived in that house for twenty years. She knew how to work the thermostat. She didn't suffer from Alzheimer's or dementia. She had been trying to reach me to ask me to come home and fix it.

You see, the heat was making her sick. With the summer temperature and all the medications she was taking plus the chemo, I have no doubt she felt terribly ill. She didn't know what else to do when she couldn't reach me, so she called the fire department for help. They had gotten there within minutes. One of the firemen walked over to the thermostat and switched it off with no problem. She said she was okay and not to worry about her.

After I got home, Mom swore to me again that she had tried repeatedly to turn it off. She said that after the fireman got the heater turned off, he went to turn on the air conditioner, but of course, it didn't work. Mom had explained our situation to them and said we couldn't afford to replace it. They listened for a minute or two, then went on their way.

That night was another scorcher. It was hot for me, and I could only imagine what my mom was going through.

The following day, the doorbell rang. I went downstairs to see who was at the door. I discovered a miracle waiting on the other side when I opened the door. Fire Department had fire trucks, emergency vehicles, and much more. There were work trucks from TLC Plumbing and a crane.

And a brand-new air conditioner.

A fireman explained that all the services and the new AC were being provided free of charge just because they wanted to help my mom. They didn't have TV cameras or newspaper reporters to cover the event. They didn't want any fanfare. The plumbing company wasn't looking for free advertising (though I'll give it to them now—TLC Plumbing is the best and if you're anywhere near Albuquerque, turn to them for all your plumbing, HVAC, and electrical needs!). These people, from both the fire department at TLC, simply felt moved to help a sick woman, a community member. Wow! God is unbelievable! He used the people of Albuquerque, Bernalillo County, and the state of New Mexico to pour out His blessings on my mom that day. That is why we are known as *The Land of Enchantment.* God saw to it that her needs were met, and Mom got to spend the last summer of her life in her own home, in cool comfort.

Do you think it was all just a series of coincidences? Or do you believe God's hand was on everything that happened that day? I think God made the heater come on for no logical reason, during that one, single hour my phone was turned off. I believe God gave my mom the idea to call the fire department, and then He sent the right people over to her house and put it in their hearts to help her. How else can I explain what happened that day than to say that God performed a miracle?

You could say my mom shouldn't have gambled away all her money, that she should have saved it for such an emergency. And yet God saw fit to bless her. Mom loved God and had complete faith in Him, but she didn't ask Him to give her a new air conditioner. With my new understanding, I know that God created this miracle in her life not just to bless her but so that I would someday share this story with all of you. And in my telling you of God's love, kindness, mercy, and power, you could experience hope and become willing to put your trust in Him. God is always good, whether or not we choose to believe it. And God is always working for the highest good of all.

Go ahead. Request away. Use your God Box so God can bless you in ways you never saw coming. What you ask for is between you and your God, so use your discretion. Place your God Box where you can see it to remind yourself and others who are really in control.

Clean out your God Box periodically. Throw away the requests God has granted and leave the ones He is still working on. Add new things that come up in your daily life. Believe and feel the power of God working in and through and for you.

Share what you have found and experienced with others, trusting in God and your God Box. God wants each of us to have a life worth living. He wants His children to experience love and happiness. God will meet all our needs. He wants us to experience Heaven here on earth through friendships with others and fellowship with Him. God wants us to be safe and free and to have peace and serenity. How do I know? God told me (but that's a subject for another book).

All the glory goes to God.

I will give all my glory to those who help others.

God

Sign up for our newsletter to read more stories of people's life-altering experiences with their God Boxes! Newsletter subscribers will also have early access to our new line of God Boxes before they go on sale to the public. Email us at the following address, and we will gladly add you to our family:

manifestwithgodnow@gmail.com

About the Author

Mark Martinez, Author and Advocate

Mark Martinez, an Albuquerque, New Mexico resident, shares his life with his wife, Christie, and their seven beloved canine companions. While many might dub his neighborhood "The Warzone" due to its reputation for trouble, drugs, and danger, Mark sees something different. He sees a community in need of compassion and support.

With over four years of sobriety under his belt, Mark is passionate about extending a helping hand to those grappling with addiction. His transformative journey from a twelve-time convicted felon to a man of positive change is a testament to the power of redemption.

Once a part of the problem, Mark has become a vital part of the solution. His remarkable transformation has not only affected his life but has also brought him into the circles of judges, police officers, and individuals from all walks of life. Mark's story serves as a beacon of hope, proving that even the most challenging circumstances can lead to a life dedicated to making a difference.

Through his writing and advocacy work, Mark continues to inspire others to overcome adversity and embrace a path of healing and renewal. His dedication to his community and his unwavering beliefs in the potential for change and God exemplify the remarkable journey of a man who has turned his life around.

Please consider writing a review.

Your reviews guide fellow readers and inspire and remind others that

there is hope in the world.